West Su

A DOG WALKER'S GUIDE

David Weller

COUNTRYSIDE BOOKS
NEWBURY BERKSHIRE

First published 2015

COUNTRYSIDE BOOKS
3 Catherine Road
Newbury, Berkshire
RG14 7NA

To view our complete range of books,
please visit us at
www.countrysidebooks.co.uk

A CIP record for this book is available from the British Library.

ISBN 978 1 84674 332 0

Photographs by the author

Cover picture supplied by
Roger Evans

Produced through The Letterworks Ltd., Reading
Typeset by Jean Cussons Typesetting, Diss, Norfolk
Printed by Berforts Information Press, Oxford

Contents

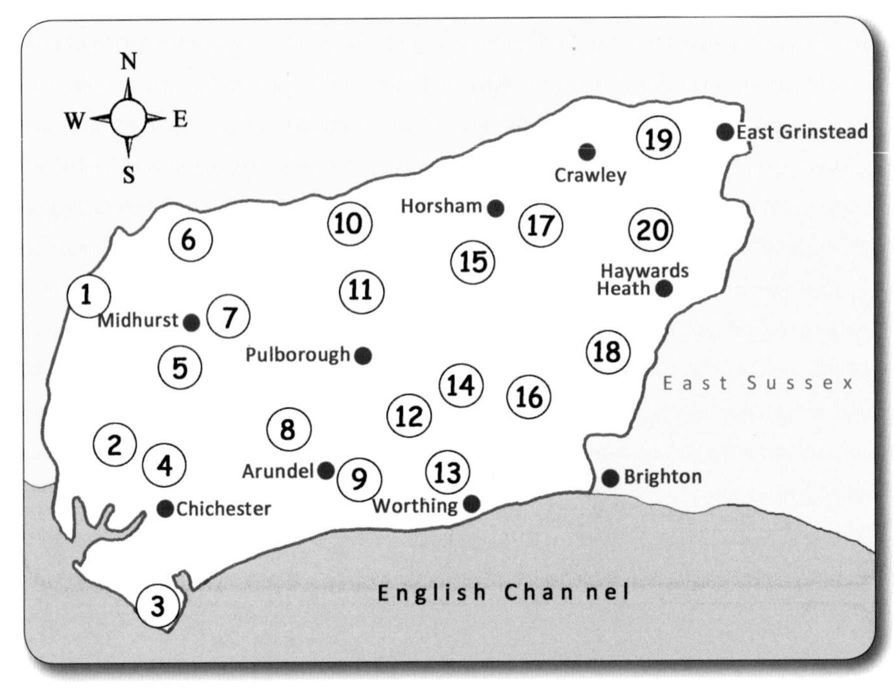

Area map showing location of the walks.

PUBLISHER'S NOTE

We hope that you obtain considerable enjoyment from this book. Although at the time of publication all routes followed public rights of way or permitted paths, diversion orders can be made and permissions withdrawn.

We cannot, of course, be held responsible for such diversion orders and any inaccuracies in the text which result from these or any other changes to the routes, nor any damage which might result from walkers trespassing on private property. We are anxious though that all details covering the walks are kept up to date and would therefore welcome information from readers which would be relevant to future editions.

The simple sketch maps that accompany the walks in the book are based on notes made by the author whilst checking out the routes on the ground. For the benefit of a proper map, however, we do recommend that you purchase the relevant Ordnance Survey sheet covering your walk. The Ordnance Survey maps are widely available, especially through booksellers and local newsagents.

INTRODUCTION

I know dog walkers generally stick to the same well-walked routes because of the fear of the unknown; stiles too difficult for the larger dog, getting lost, busy roads, or being confronted by a herd of cattle. Well, how about trying somewhere new where those fears are largely eliminated?

I grew up with a dog as a young boy and since those distant days, my family and I have had the great pleasure of owning many wonderful four-legged companions. What a joy it is to be accompanied by man's best friend when walking through the lovely West Sussex countryside – I can't think of a better way of seeing it.

These 20 good circular routes cover a wide range of landscapes; from the high chalk grasslands of the South Downs studded with wildflowers, to ancient woodland in the Low Weald where the summer sun filters down through the leaf canopy above, then, in total contrast, the shingle beach of unpretentious Selsey on the South Coast – what a feast!

I have recommended dog-friendly pubs along the way or nearby but, personally, I especially enjoy an al fresco snack at one of the many scenic picnic spots these walks pass. To this aim I always carry a small rucksack with a flask of coffee and a sandwich for me and, more importantly, a bottle of water and drinking bowl for my canine friend. I recommend you wear walking boots as they offer grip in wet conditions and give good ankle support on uneven ground.

I have drawn sketch maps and each one has numbered points that correspond to a paragraph in the walk directions, but I always recommend carrying the relevant Ordnance Survey map so that you have a better understanding of the area you are walking in.

Finally, I do hope you and your dog enjoy these 20 lovely circuits – happy walking!

David Weller

All routes have been approved by Paddy – a walkies enthusiast!

ADVICE FOR DOG WALKERS

The countryside is a wonderful place for both you and your dog to walk and exercise in, but there are a few things that should be remembered. Although you may think you understand your own dog, they are basically predatory animals with an instinctive behaviour pattern, some of which has been developed by man so they can 'work'.

Livestock: Some routes go through fields of sheep, which are hard to avoid in the South Downs National Park, so at these times always keep your dog on the lead. As much as possible, I have avoided routes through fields that are home to cows or horses but, over time, usage may change. If cows are chanced upon, remember to never walk between them and their calves. Cows can be inquisitive and come too close to you; if this happens, drop the lead and make your way out of the field – dogs are faster than cows and are well able to look after themselves.

Ground nesting birds: Keep your dog on a lead in nature reserves and on heathland during the breeding season of 1st March to 31st July as this is a particularly vulnerable time for ground nesting birds. Adult birds will abandon their nests if they are disturbed by a dog. The nests become vulnerable to predators and chicks can die from cold or lack of food.

Bridleways: Many of these routes are along wide tracks that are shared with horse riders and cyclists. Your dog may never have seen a horse before and could react with a mixture of fear or nervousness, which may turn to defensive aggression. Alternatively, they will want to chase and play – behaviour that the horse is unlikely to understand. So, if a horse rider is encountered, please put your dog on its lead and stand back to allow them to pass. With cyclists, to avoid accidents, common sense dictates the same advice.

Dog mess and plastic bags: If you are in an area where dog bins are provided, then always 'bag it and bin it' but, as most of these routes are through countryside that is much less well equipped, get a stick and flick it off the path into the undergrowth where it will not be trodden on and will decompose. Please do not bag it and throw it into the bushes. Plastic bags do not decompose. If eaten by an animal, the plastic cannot be digested and stays in their gut, eventually killing them. The animal dies and decays, but not the plastic which is then freed back into the environment to carry on killing other wildlife.

Lost dog: Try to keep your dog within sight at all times. By law your dog must have a collar and identity tag but it is also a good idea to have it micro chipped. Even the best behaved dogs can become lost at times and no owner – or dog – wants that to happen!

Vets: If your dog is injured or becomes unwell during one of these walks, details of the nearest vets are given for each walk in the *Dog factors* box.

Ticks: It is a good idea to check your dog for ticks after a walk, especially if you've been in a wooded area or near bracken. If you find a tick, remove it as soon as possible. Use tweezers, or better still get a special tick remover from a pet shop. Grasp the tick as close as possible to the skin. Then pull the tick straight out without squeezing or twisting it. You can apply products to your dog to prevent ticks and fleas.

1

Durford Heath and Rogate Common

Passing through Rogate Common.

This lovely circuit will be every dog's delight! The easy-to-follow route near the Hampshire border begins in the magnificent woodland of Durford Heath, where dogs can run around freely, and for the most part is far away from roads. The woodland is wonderful and the peace and quietness it offers is only broken by the birdsong that seems to resound from every treetop. After following a wide bridleway that gradually descends between the trees, the first turning point is met at a sunken path that leads to a quiet country lane. Within a quarter of a mile the circuit leaves the lane and begins its return where, again, wide tracks are walked. Heading back, the route climbs easily and passes through the delightful woodland of Rogate Common before all too soon ending back at the car park.

Terrain

The first half of the route descends easily while the return has an almost unnoticed rise of 280 feet.

Where to park

Durford Heath National Trust car park at Hill Brow. **OS map:** Explorer 133 Haslemere and Petersfield (GR: SU 791 260).

How to get there

Hill Brow sits astride the B2070, just 2½ miles north of Petersfield. Turn east on the road signed to Rogate beside the Jolly Drover public house and after 300 yards the car park will be found beside the last house on your right.

Nearest refreshments

There is a small grassy picnic spot next to the car park; picnic along the route or visit the **Jolly Drover** where dogs are allowed in the garden. ☎ 01730 893137

The Walk

1 Leave the car park via the gate opposite its entrance and follow the broad path as it gradually descends through woodland. This path forms a section of the long distance **Sussex Border Path**. At a fork, keep to the signed bridleway.

By now you will have noticed that this is not heathland at all. It was until 150 years ago when it was planted with oaks and regularly coppiced to provide charcoal for the local iron industry.

Later the bridleway narrows as it passes between fields. At the foot of the valley ignore paths to left and right and continue ahead on the bridleway.

Dog factors

Distance: 3¾ miles.
Road walking: 400 yards of country lane without pavement.
Livestock: None, but maybe the occasional horse rider.
Stiles: None.
Nearest vets: St Peter's Vets Ltd., Mill Road, Liss GU33 7AZ
☎ 01730 894222

❷ At a right bend, leave the **Sussex Border Path** by turning left along a sunken path signed as a Public Way. Later ignore a bridleway on your left and keep to the Public Way until it ends at a small country road. Go ahead along the road and pass **Slade Farm**.

The Sussex Border Path follows the inland boundary of what was once the Kingdom of the South Saxons; now modern-day East and West Sussex. The 150 mile route was first devised in 1983. It begins in the east by the Kent border at Rye, before

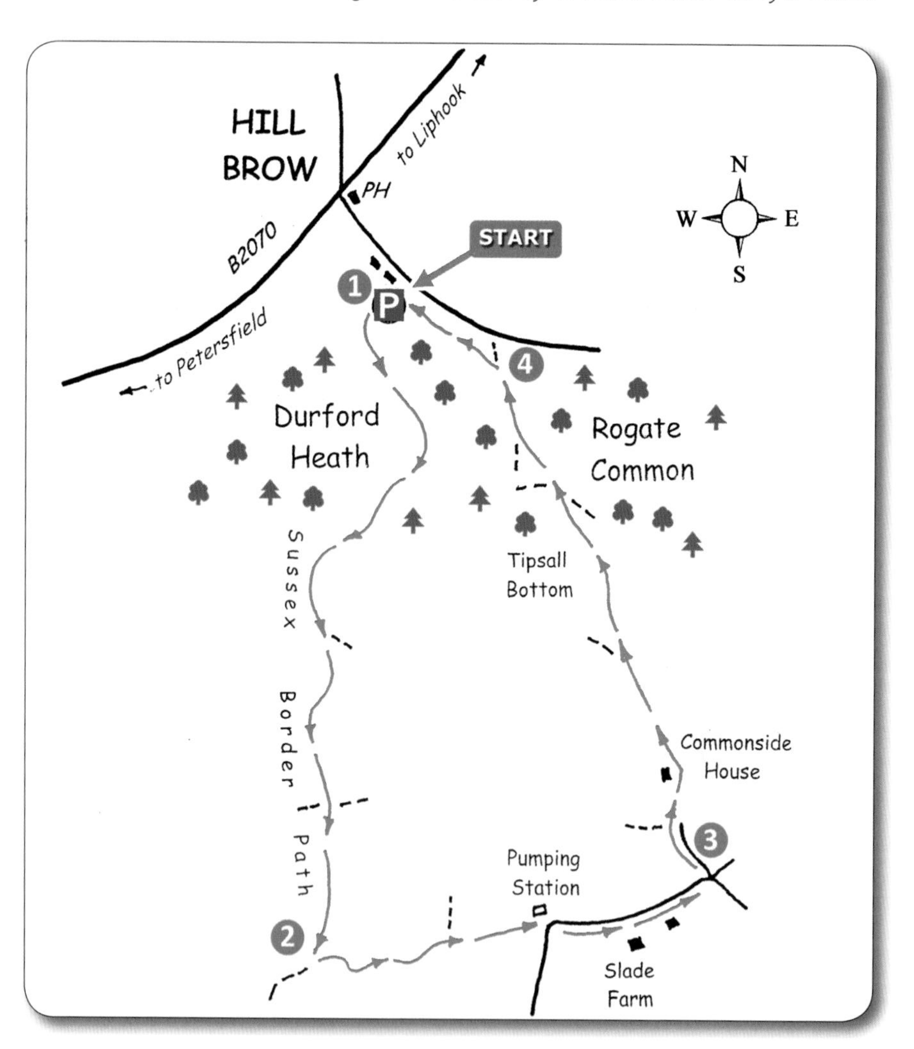

crossing the more remote and unspoilt areas of south-east England to Emsworth, on the Hampshire border.

3 After passing thatched **Little Slade** continue for 90 yards, then turn left at a small road junction. At the gate to **Commonside House** ignore a footpath on your left and walk ahead on the bridleway along the drive. Pass the front of the house and follow the bridleway leftwards and soon enter woodland. When the bridleway divides by a large clearing, ignore the left fork and maintain direction ahead on the rising bridleway.

4 With a road 120 yards ahead of you and a two-bar wooden vehicle barrier to your left, go left on a permissive footpath, ignoring paths to left and right, to rejoin the car park.

Can you see a face there?

2

Stoughton Down and Lyecommon

A pretty corner of Stoughton.

What a wonderful dog walk this circuit is! Almost the whole of this great route is along easy-to-follow wide tracks where dogs have the freedom to roam, run or sniff away to their hearts' content and, as you would expect of the South Downs National Park, the scenery is quite stunning. The route begins by passing through lovely woodland above Greatdean Bottom to reach the heights of Stoughton Down where the Monarch's Way and panoramic views are met. The long distance path then leads you into the valley below and through the pretty village of Stoughton before you come to some more peaceful woodland and the furthest point of the route at Lyecommon. The way then makes its return on wide tracks alongside arable fields and through more shady woodland – a real treat on a summer's day.

Terrain

Hilly, but well within the capability of anyone of average fitness.

Where to park

Stoughton Down car park. **OS map:** Explorer 120 Chichester, South Harting and Selsey (GR: SU 815 125).

How to get there

Stoughton Down is 5 miles north-west of Chichester. From the B2141, half a mile west of Chilgrove, turn west on a lane signed to East Marden. Fork left at the village pump and follow the lane for 1¾ miles to reach the car park on your left.

Nearest refreshments

There is a grassy area beside the car park, ideal for picnics. The route passes the dog-friendly **Hare and Hounds** pub in Stoughton where a good selection of lunchtime fare and an inviting garden are to be found. ☎ 02392 631433.

The Walk

1. From the left side of the car park, pass a vehicle barrier and go ahead on a wide track alongside woodland. As the track bends right, ignore a left-forking bridleway and keep to the stony track as it begins to rise through majestic woodland. Ignore the occasional track to left and right and remain on this track as it gains height to meet a crossing bridleway near the crest of the hill.

Dog factors

Distance: 6 miles.
Road walking: In total, ½ mile of country lanes without pavements and one country lane to cross.
Livestock: None but you may meet the occasional horse rider.
Stiles: 2, both easy for all but the very largest of dogs.
Nearest vets: Alphapet Veterinary Clinic, Oldwick Farm, West Stoke Road, Lavant, Chichester PO18 9AA
☎ 01243 528899

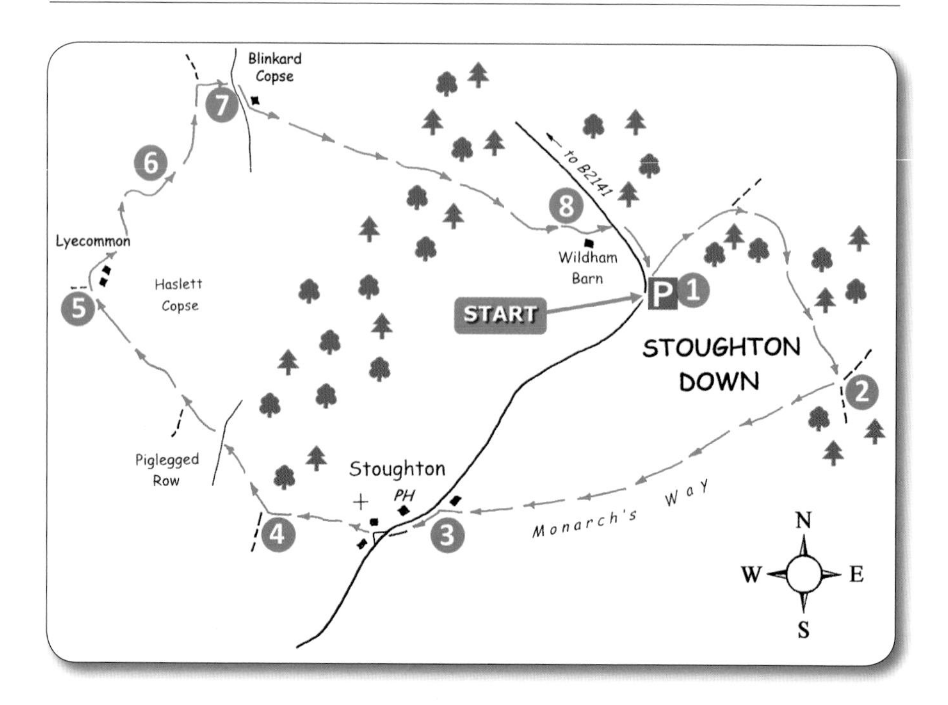

❷ Turn right here on the signed **Monarch's Way** long distance path where soon you will have magnificent panoramic views. Keep to this lovely downhill track between fields until it finally passes farm buildings and ends at a village road by a cluster of fine houses.

❸ Turn left and follow the road through **Stoughton** village, passing the **Hare and Hounds** pub. At the tiny village green, fork right to a telephone box and then follow an uphill stony bridleway between houses. When nearing the top of the rise, ignore a wide track forking right and remain on the signed **Monarch's Way**.

❹ At a directional post on a dip slope where the **Monarch's Way** goes left, leave the long distance path by continuing ahead on the bridleway. After exiting woodland the path follows the edge of a field to reach a lane. Cross to the bridleway opposite and continue ahead through rising woodland, soon ignoring a signed bridleway on your left. After exiting woodland the way continues along a ribbon of trees to meet a T-junction.

❺ Turn right here on a signed public footpath along a track where you soon pass a couple of well-sited houses at **Lyecommon**. Cross a stile beside a gate and press on along a forestry track. At a fork, go right on the signed footpath and at a second fork by a large beech tree, fork left.

6 When the track leaves woodland it continues along the right side of a large arable field where you should ignore a track forking right. At the field end go ahead in woodland and after 100 yards ignore a footpath ahead of you and turn right along the track that ends at a gate and stile at a lane.

7 Turn right along the lane and soon turn left on a signed bridleway along a track beside a house. Remain on this track as it passes through woodland before continuing alongside an arable field. At the end of the field, go through woodland to meet a directional post in 20 yards. Press on ahead here along the signed bridleway and ignore crossing paths and tracks.

8 Finally, after going downhill, a house named **Wildham Barn** is reached. Fork left along its drive to meet with a lane. Turn right along the lane to soon reach the car park and the end of this really good walk.

A wonderful downland view from the Monarch's Way as it descends over Stoughton Down.

3

Selsey and Pagham Harbour

Everyone enjoys a stroll along the prom.

This interesting, varied and easy-to-follow route is a treat – especially for dogs as towards its end they can cool off with a splash in the sea on a hot day (or even when it isn't). Beginning at Selsey's East Beach, the route goes along the promenade for a short distance before heading inland along a quiet residential road. After turning along a farm track, the way continues between level fields where salad leaves are cultivated by a large producer. The turning point comes at Church Norton where a few yards beyond the route, Grade I listed St Wilfrid's Chapel can be explored. The route turns and, after passing the earthwork of an 11th-century castle, joins the shore of Pagham Harbour Nature Reserve. Now heading towards the sea, the way comes to the shingle of the farthest reaches of East Beach, from where it begins the return to the car park. Dogs have the freedom of this end of the beach all year round but where it is backed by the promenade, summertime dog restrictions apply from 1st May until 30th September.

Terrain
Level.

Where to park
East Beach pay and display car park in Selsey. **OS map:** Explorer 120 Chichester, South Harting and Selsey (GR: SZ 866 934).

How to get there
Selsey is 8 miles south of Chichester on the B2145. As you enter Selsey, turn left at the first roundabout signed to the car park. At a T-junction turn left and later fork right by a parade of shops. At a T-junction with Beach Road, turn left to reach the car park on your left.

Nearest refreshments
Beside the car park is a seasonal café while further along the seafront behind the lifeboat station in Albion Road is the dog-friendly **Lifeboat Inn**. ☎ 01243 603501

The Walk

1. From the far end of the car park go up to the **promenade** and turn leftwards along it for a short distance. Look out for a plaque on your left commemorating the assembling of the Mulberry Harbours here for D-Day during the Second World War. Turn left here; now go ahead and follow **Drift Road** until it bends sharply left.

Dog factors

Distance: 3½ miles.
Road walking: ¼ mile along a quiet residential road with a pavement and grass verge and ¼ mile along a cul-de-sac country lane without pavement.
Livestock: None.
Stiles: None.
Nearest vets: Alphapet Veterinary Clinic, Northleigh Farm, Main Road, Birdham, Chichester PO20 7BY
☎ 01243 513514

The Mulberry Harbours of the Second World War were an essential requirement for the D-Day landings. Construction of the artificial harbours began during 1943 and it was such a massive project that it took over 300 civil engineering companies and more than 40,000 personnel to complete them. Although building the caissons, over 200 in all and weighing up to 1,600 tons each, was undertaken mainly by companies along the rivers Thames and Clyde, smaller sections were manufactured in Richborough in Kent, Southsea and Southampton. Selsey was the point at which they were all stored prior to being towed across the English Channel and put together off the Normandy coast.

2 At this sharp bend, turn right and continue along a farm track to meet a junction of tracks by **Park Farm**. Go ahead on a public footpath between a house and farm buildings and press on along a concrete track between fields where salad crops are grown. Ignore a driveway on your left and when the concrete drive finally bends left, maintain direction ahead along a cart track between fields.

3 At the end of the field on your right, pass by a gate and go leftwards on a signed footpath, with a large arable field to your right. At the field end, ignore a footpath signed rightwards and press on ahead to meet a farm drive. Continue ahead, passing **Greenlease Farm**, and remain on this drive until it ends at a country lane.

Enjoying the sea breeze!

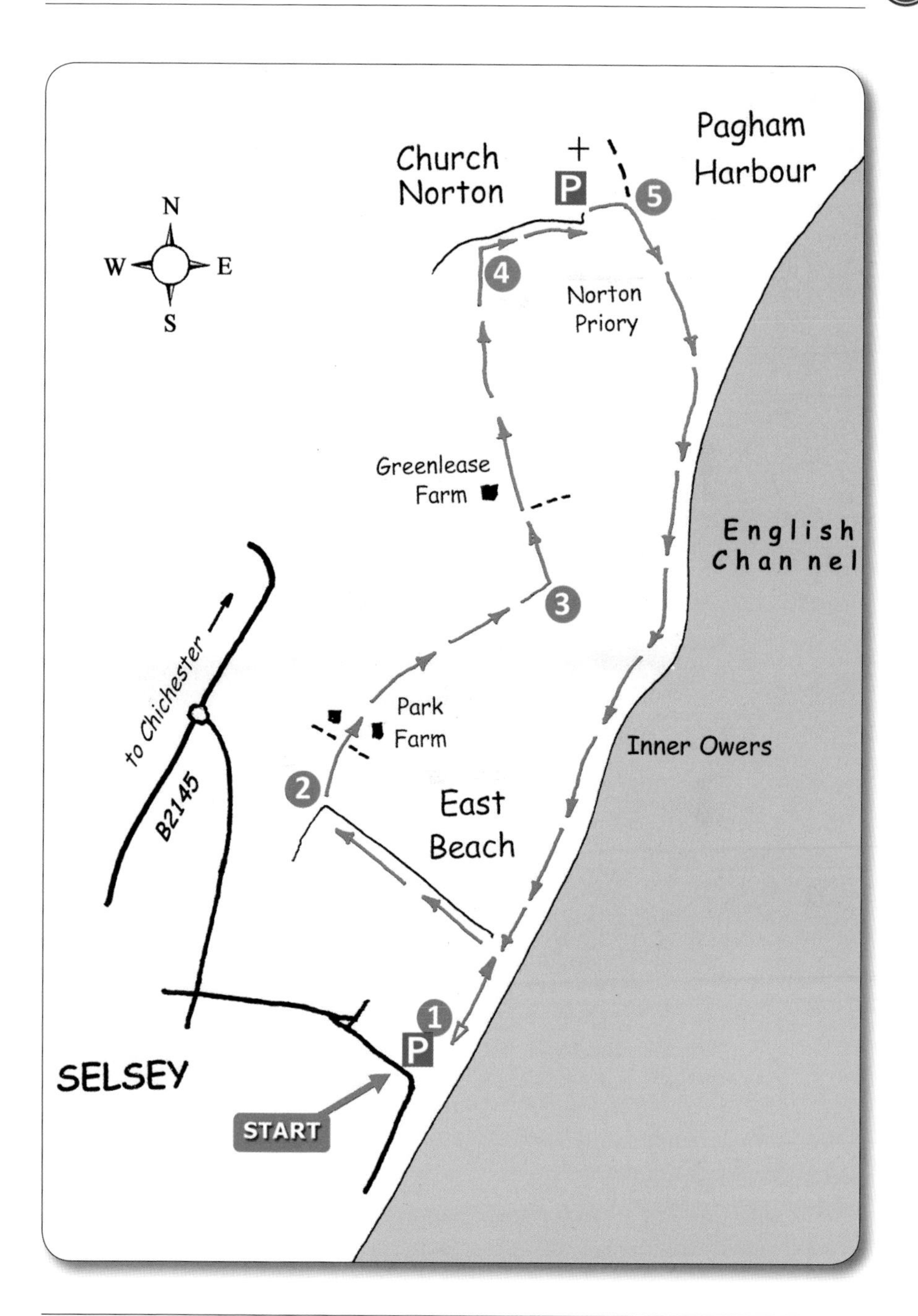
Pagham Harbour
Church Norton
P
5
N
W
E
S
4
Norton Priory
Greenlease Farm
English Channel
3
to Chichester
Park Farm
Inner Owers
2
B2145
East Beach
1
P
SELSEY
START

4. Turn right along this little quiet lane that ends at the car park of **St Wilfrid's Chapel**. Turn right in the car park; pass by a gate and the earthworks of an **11th-century castle** to soon reach the shore of **Pagham Harbour Nature Reserve**.

5. Turn right along the shore to reach the shingle banks of the **Inner Owers** where dogs have the freedom to enjoy themselves at the water's edge. Continuing along the shingle or along an unmade track lined with eclectic seaside houses will bring you back to **East Beach** (and dog restrictions) to complete this splendid circuit. In summer, leave the beach for the last stretch and walk back along the promenade.

St Wilfrid's Chapel in rural Church Norton is just a remnant of a much larger Norman church. All that remains is the 13th-century chancel, standing alone in its large churchyard. From the 13th century to the mid 1860s, this was the site of the parish church. But it was decided to dismantle the church and move it to the centre of Selsey, to serve the growing population. It is worth looking inside the chapel to see a stunning, modern stained glass window installed in the 1980s. It shows a local nature reserve and if you look carefully, you can spot moles, stoats, foxes, a woodpecker, avocet and shelduck

East Lavant and St Roche's Hill

A walk through stunning landscape.

This is a spectacular walk at any time of the year but especially good during early summer when wildflowers are plentiful and in bloom. For almost the entire route, dogs will have the freedom to roam off the lead and explore the sights and scents for themselves. After leaving East Lavant's pretty village green, the route follows a bridleway for over two miles through lovely scenery to reach Great Combes on the outskirts of West Dean. Here the way turns onto a wide track that soon goes through shady woodland on a none-too-difficult climb to reach the top of St Roche's Hill and a great picnic spot. From this vantage point with its panoramic views, the way heads back to East Lavant along a wide track that gently descends between banks dotted with pyramidal orchids in season while ahead there are great views towards Chichester's cathedral spire in the distance.

Terrain

One steady rise of 280 feet that will not trouble anyone of average fitness – otherwise fairly level or downhill.

Where to park

Layby in Sheepwash Lane, East Lavant just west of the village green. **OS map:** Explorer 120 Chichester, South Harting and Selsey (GR: SU 859 084)

How to get there

East Lavant is 2¾ miles north of Chichester, off the A286. Heading north, from a roundabout on the A286 at Mid Lavant, turn east along Pook Lane, signed to Lavant Memorial Hall. Pass the hall and at the end of the village green turn sharp left into Sheepwash Lane. The layby is just past the green. Alternative parking alongside the green.

Nearest refreshments

St Roche's Hill is a good picnic spot or, near the end of the route on your return to East Lavant, the way passes the **Royal Oak**, which offers a good selection of lunchtime food. Small to medium sized dogs on leads are welcome in the small bar, while all sizes can enjoy the outside seating area. ☎ 01243 527434

The Walk

1. From the layby, walk back to the **village green** and when halfway along it, turn left on a signed bridleway along the drive to **Staple House Farm**. As the drive turns into the grounds, press on ahead on the bridleway. Along the way ignore two left forks and remain on the main path for 1¼ miles until a gate is reached.

Dog factors

Distance: 5 miles.
Road walking: ½ mile with some pavements.
Livestock: Sheep in two fields (see point 2) plus the occasional horse rider.
Stiles: None.
Nearest vets: Alphapet Veterinary Clinic, Oldwick Farm, West Stoke Road, Lavant, Chichester PO18 9AA ☎ 01243 528899

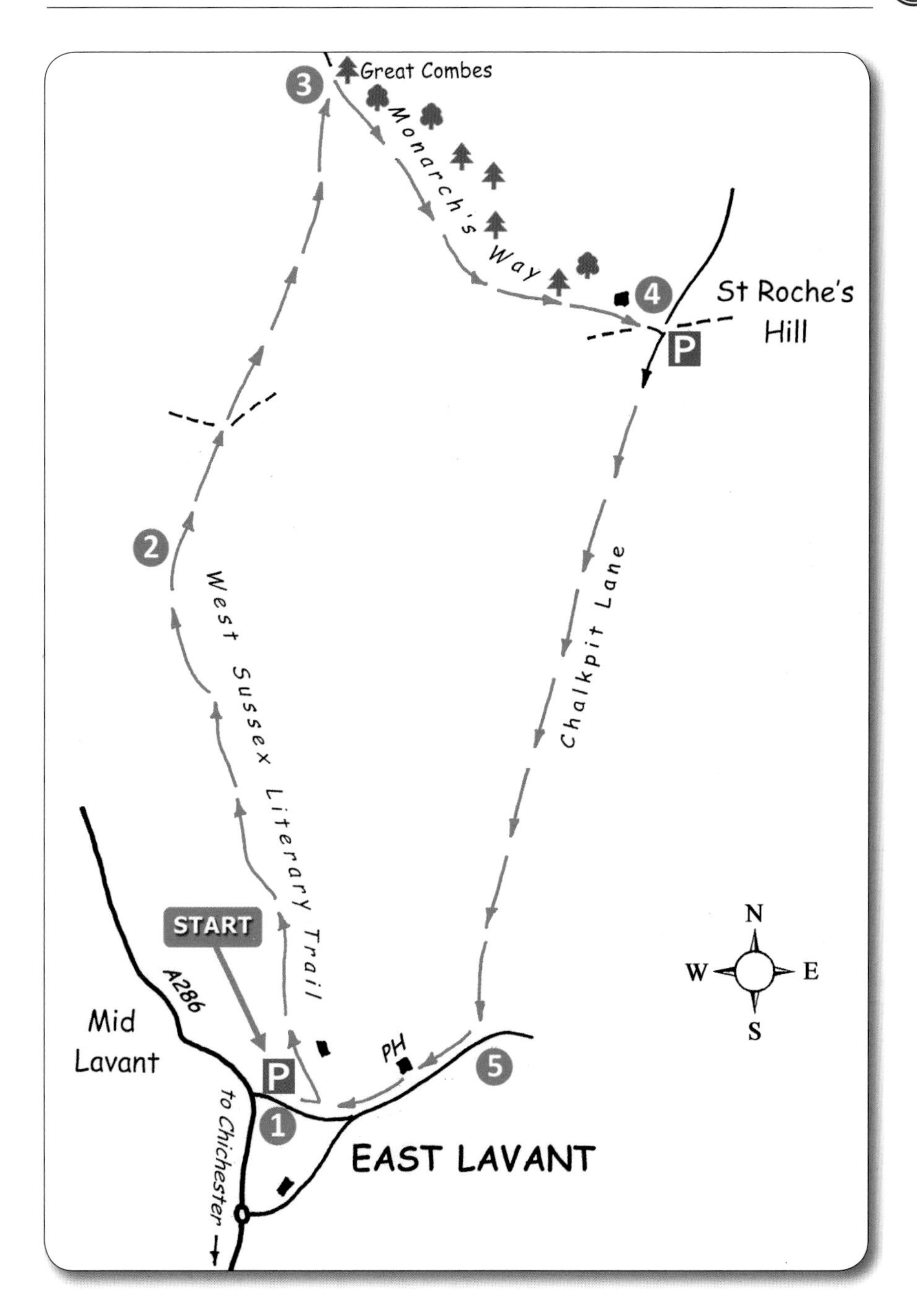
Great Combes
Monarch's Way
St Roche's Hill
P
West Sussex Literary Trail
Chalkpit Lane
START
A286
Mid Lavant
P
PH
to Chichester
EAST LAVANT
N
W
E
S
1
2
3
4
5

The 55-mile West Sussex Literary Trail opened in 2007. It begins in Horsham and passes interesting towns and villages where prominent playwrights and poets once lived, before finally ending in the cathedral city of Chichester.

2. Pass through the gate and enter a sheep meadow in **West Dean Estate**. Go ahead along the left side of this and a second sheep meadow where obviously dogs must be on leads. Along the way ignore a crossing bridleway. At the end of these meadows pass through a gate and continue on a fenced path to meet a wide stony track by a flint wall.

Pretty cottages in East Lavant.

3 Turn right here and follow the rising track as it passes alongside an arable field before entering shady woodland. After exiting woodland beside a large Georgian house, a T-junction is met. Go left here to soon reach a tarmac road at **Seven Points car park** on **St Roche's Hill**.

4 Turn right, pass the side of the car park and continue on a wide downhill chalky track that, without further directions being necessary, brings you back to **East Lavant** in 1½ miles.

This wide, downhill chalky track is unsurprisingly called 'Chalkpit Lane', a modern name for what is probably an ancient Neolithic track way. There are the remains of chalk workings in the fields to the west of the track, created by lime burners who endeavoured to improve the poor chalky soils for agriculture. Once, chalk caves (now filled in) existed on the western side of the track; some believe they could have been dug as early as 2,000 years ago to give shelter to shepherds and their flocks during Roman times.

5 Turn right alongside the village street where you will pass the **Royal Oak**. At the **village green** fork right along **Sheepwash Lane** to reach the layby.

It is worth spending some time in the charming village of East Lavant. The 18th-century village pub is said to be haunted. Two smugglers murdered a Revenue man at this pub 200 years ago during a gunfight. Since that time, on occasions a tall bearded man, dressed in old fashioned clothing, has been seen in the bedrooms upstairs, and heard climbing the creaking staircase. The village is also known for its 'drinking pig'. In the 1940s, a local farmer gave the runt of the litter some beer to help build it up. A newspaper heard about it and sent a reporter to investigate. Unfortunately, by the time the reporter arrived, the beer had fattened up the pig enough for it to be sent to slaughter. Not wanting to miss out on some publicity, another pig was quickly found. The newspaper photo was taken showing the farmer with his 'drinking pig', the pub landlord and his family, all proudly standing by the bar.

5

Cocking Down and Bepton Down

The cool shade of a cart track as the route leaves Cocking Down.

This is a varied and fairly energetic walk but well worth the effort. The route begins by following the South Downs Way long distance path on a fairly steady rise to the top of Cocking Down and along the way the views across the adjoining countryside are panoramic and quite stunning. Having reached the hilltop, the way turns north and begins to descend gently on a wide track through indigenous woodland by Bepton Down and Stead Combe where it meets up with Henley Lane – no more than a grassy cart track nowadays. Later the way passes through Crypt Farm before making the short climb back to the long distance path from where it is an easy stroll to the car park. The route is far away from roads so dogs will enjoy their freedom and the chance to spend time sniffing the multitude of scents the countryside offers.

Terrain

The rise of 400 feet over 1¼ miles at the beginning would be unlikely to trouble a person or dog of average fitness.

Where to park

Cocking Hill car park. **OS map:** Explorer 120 Chichester, South Harting and Selsey (GR: SU 875 167).

How to get there

Cocking is 3 miles south of Midhurst, on the A286. The car park is off the main road ½ mile south of the village and can easily be missed. The car park entrance is at the top of the hill beside a bus stop on the western side of the road.

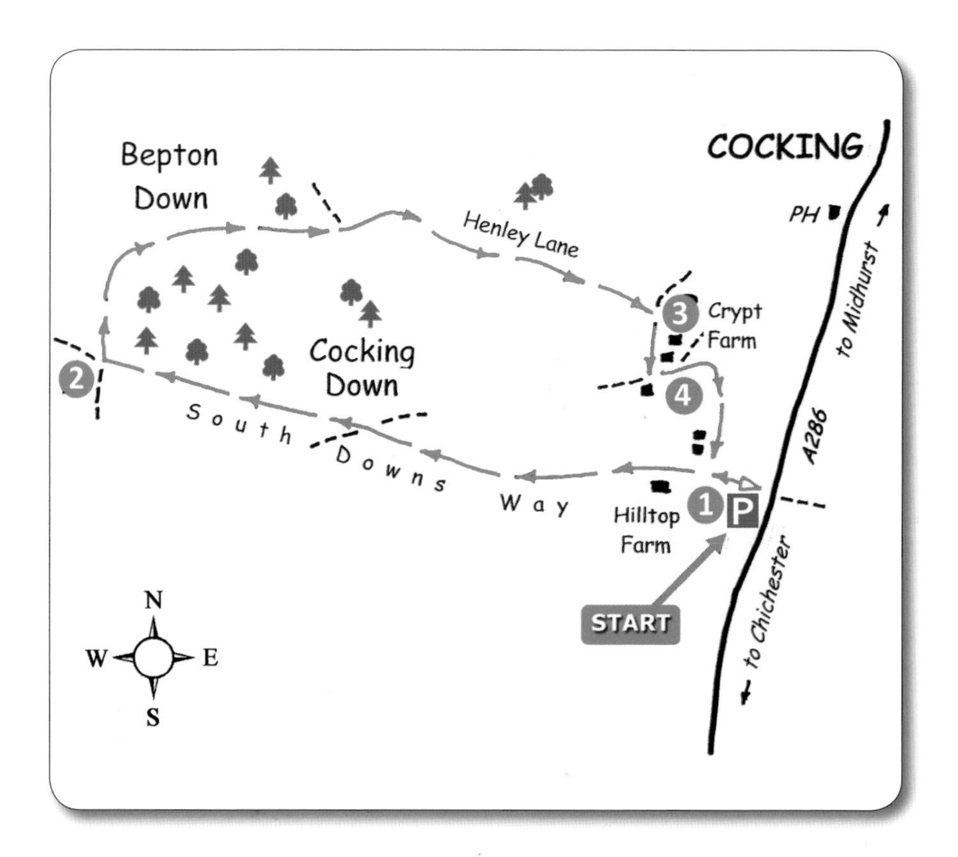

Dog factors

Distance: 3¼ miles.
Road walking: None.
Livestock: Well-fenced cattle, but during spring and summer there are many hundreds of young pheasants roaming the fields and tracks and so dogs should always be kept under control.
Stiles: None.
Nearest vets: Woodland Veterinary Centre, Grange Road, Midhurst GU29 9LT ☎ 01730 814321

Nearest refreshments

Dogs are allowed in the garden of the **Bluebell Inn** on the A286 in Cocking (☎ 01730 810200) or you will find many enticing spots for picnics along the route.

The Walk

1. Leave the car park at its northern end and turn left along the **South Downs Way** long distance path. Soon pass the buildings of **Hilltop Farm** and press on ahead along the stony track. As you climb higher, ignore a bridleway to the left and right by a large chalk ball and keep ahead.

The South Downs Way is a 100 mile National Trail from Winchester, once the seat of the first king of England, Alfred the Great, across rolling countryside to Eastbourne, in East Sussex. It takes the walker through the South Downs National Park, along ancient trackways and farm tracks, passing pretty villages and the remains of Roman villas.

2. At the top of the hill a Restricted Byway is met. Turn right here along it and soon enter shady woodland where the track offers easy walking and shade in summer. Later ignore a Restricted Byway on your left and press on ahead along the grassy track known as **Henley Lane**, lined by hedgerows.

3. The track ends at a T-junction where you should turn right on another Restricted Byway, a little narrower this time. At a tennis court, turn right alongside a garden before soon turning left to meet a cart track. Turn left and pass between the buildings of **Crypt Farm**.

4 At the end of a barn, ignore a Restricted Byway forking left and press on ahead on the one signed to the **South Downs Way**. After a short climb, cross a farm track and pass a couple of cottages to rejoin the long distance path where a left turn soon brings you back to the car park.

This carved chalk ball measures 2 metres across and marks the beginning of a walk called 'The Chalk Stones Trail'. The 5-mile trail is marked by 12 more carved chalk balls and was created by Andy Goldsworthy, an environmental artist. Goldsworthy creates his sculptures from natural materials, like leaves and ice, with some of his work lasting for just a few hours. The chalk stones were installed in 2002 and have gradually discoloured over time and are very slowly fading into the landscape. The stones were excavated from a quarry in West Sussex then roughly chiselled by the artist into balls.

6

Fernhurst and its environs

The Red Lion overlooks the village green.

This good dog walk begins in the centre of Fernhurst before setting off eastwards and passing St Margaret's church to meet the idyllic village green and the Red Lion pub. A short stroll from here along a country lane brings you to a footpath that leads you easily through woodland and across fields on a mainly fenced path around the southern reaches of the village. After crossing the A286 the route delves deeper into the countryside as it follows a bridleway through Whitter's Copse to meet its next turning point by the majestic woodland of Amon's Copse. From here the route makes its return by first passing Lower Hawksfold before soon joining the magnificent driveway of Hawksfold Farm, which leads you back to the village to complete this delightfully rural circuit.

Terrain

Fairly level.

Where to park

The car park in Crossfield off Vann Road. **OS map:** Explorer 133 Haslemere and Petersfield (GR: SU 895 284).

How to get there

Fernhurst is 3 miles south of Haslemere, on the A286. At the crossroads in the centre of the village go west along Vann Road for 120 yards before turning left into Crossfield.

Nearest refreshments

The dog-friendly **Red Lion** pub by the village green serves good light lunches and is passed along the route. Dogs will enjoy sunning themselves in the spacious outside eating area, or if they prefer, a snooze in the shade of the bar. Wherever they choose they are welcome. ☎ 01428 643112

The Walk

1. Walk back to **Vann Road** and turn right to meet the crossroads. Cross the **A286** and press on ahead along **Church Road**. Pass by **St Margaret's church** to reach the village green where you will see the **Red Lion** pub ahead and left. Turn right along a quiet lane and soon, when it bends left, go right through a gate on a signed footpath.

2. Follow the waymarked path as it leads you through fields and woodland. At a field edge cross a stile and fork left across the field and cross a stile at the far side. Pass through a ribbon of woodland and press on ahead

Dog factors

Distance: 3¼ miles.
Road walking: ½ mile with some pavements.
Livestock: None but maybe the occasional horse rider.
Stiles: 10; all passable by dogs up to labrador size.
Nearest vets: Crofts Veterinary Surgery, Collards Lane, off Petworth Road, Haslemere GU27 2HU ☎ 01428 653056

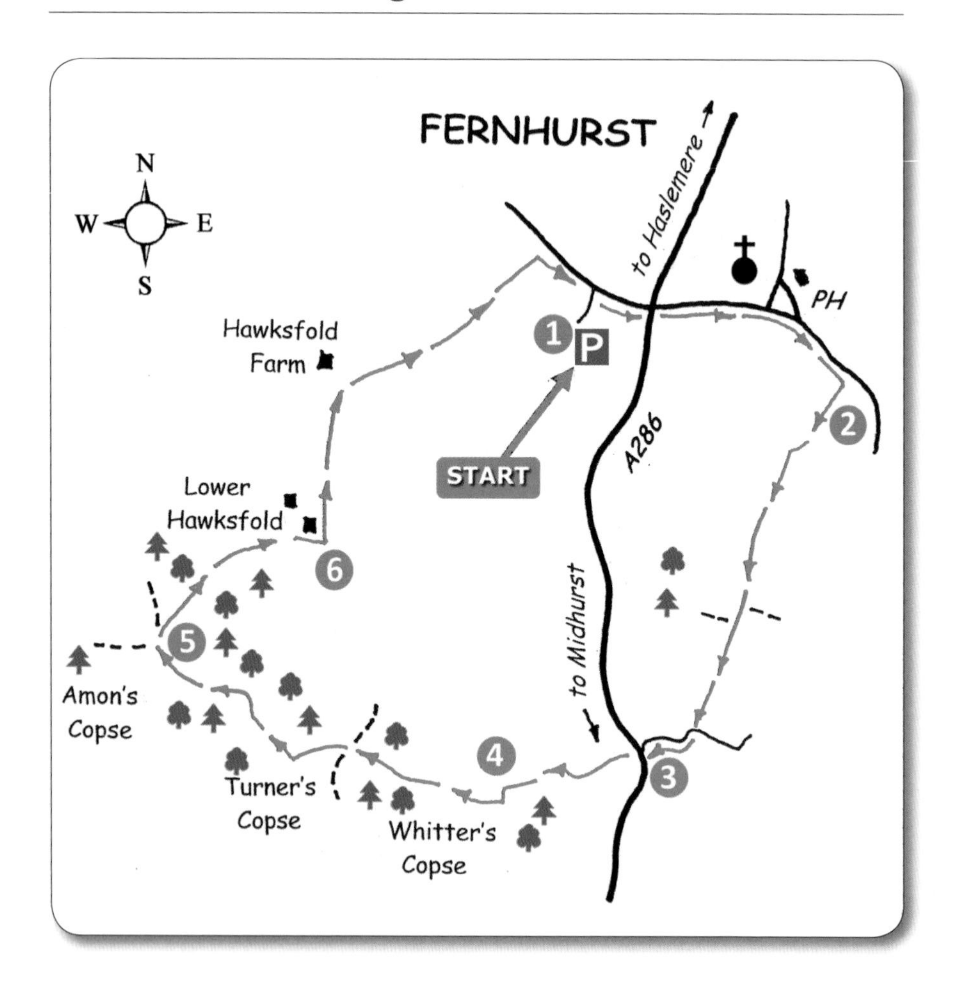

over the next field to meet a directional post. Maintain direction here on a fenced path, which ends at a small lane. Go right along the lane to meet the **A286** road.

3 Go diagonally left over the main road, with caution, to meet a gated bridleway. Follow the bridleway through a second gate and continue ahead alongside a woodland brook. At a fork, keep left on the signed bridleway and climb a low ridge.

4 With a field gate ahead of you, turn left and within yards go right between fields. When the right-hand field ends, enter woodland. Ignore a crossing path here and go ahead. Follow the bridleway when it turns right downhill and crosses a planked bridge. The track later passes between majestic pine trees and at a fork follow the bridleway right. Cross another planked bridge to meet a field edge.

5 Turn right along the field edge for 15 yards before forking right through a ribbon of woodland to meet a field. Go ahead along its right-hand edge and cross a stile in the far corner. Press on ahead along a grassy path, cross a farm bridge, go up a gully and continue right as the path becomes enclosed.

6 At the corner of a barn follow the path left and later cross a planked bridge in a dell. Continue through a kissing gate where the path becomes enclosed and meets the driveway of **Lower Hawksfold**. Go right along the drive to meet the large gates to **Hawksfold Farm**. Pass through the pedestrian gate and now follow this scenic drive to eventually rejoin **Vann Road**. A right turn alongside the road brings you back to **Crossfield** and the end of this varied circuit.

St Margaret's church at Fernhurst.

Lodsworth and Vining Copse

The dog-friendly Hollist Arms in the centre of Lodsworth village.

This super walk begins in the pretty village of Lodsworth and soon follows an old drovers' route through the peace and quiet of the countryside. The sunken tracks in this area were worn down centuries ago by the passage of countless sheep and cattle on their way to summer grazing and now form wonderful eye-level miniature nature reserves where the low sandstone cliffs and exposed tree roots provide a haven for ferns, mosses and burrowing creatures. The route is ideal for dogs as it is far from

roads and allows them untold freedom as it gradually climbs the ridge to its turning point at Bexleyhill. Returning through peaceful woodland, the way continues along woodland tracks that offer keyhole views over the surrounding countryside before all too soon ending back in Lodsworth. In the summer, you could wander down to watch the village cricket club playing at Recreation Ground, on Heath End Lane.

Terrain

Undulating.

Where to park

Park considerately at the roadside in Lodsworth village near the Hollist Arms. **OS map:** Explorer 133 Haslemere and Petersfield (GR: SU 928 231).

How to get there

Approaching on the A272, Lodsworth is signed to the north, 3 miles west of Petworth and 3 miles east of Midhurst. Follow the lane for ¾ mile to reach the centre of the village and the Hollist Arms from where the circuit begins.

Nearest refreshments

The dog-friendly 15th-century **Hollist Arms** in Lodsworth village where delicious snacks and good home-made meals are on offer. Dogs are welcome in the bar area and there is a small beer garden. The pub is open 7 days a week and specialises in seasonal English and French food. ☎ 01798 861310, Alternatively, you could buy picnic ingredients from Lodsworth Larder. This community run shop sells local artisan cheeses, delicatessen produce, cakes and pastries. ☎ 01798 861947.

Dog factors

Distance: 4¼ miles.
Road walking: In total just over ½ mile of country lane without pavement.
Livestock: None but may be the occasional horse rider.
Stiles: None.
Nearest vets: Woodland Veterinary Centre, Grange Road, Midhurst GU29 9LT
☎ 01730 814321

The Walk

1. When facing the **Hollist Arms**, walk along **Gills Lane** to its left. Continue ahead at a small road junction and later pass the **Village Hall**. At a left bend by the gate to **Heath End Farm**, continue ahead on a signed bridleway.

2. When a T-junction is met, turn right along a slowly rising sunken bridleway. At the top of the rise you come to a cart track by a paddock. Press on ahead along the track and soon go over a crossing track and pass by the gate to **Vining Farm**. Continue until you meet an open grassy area with a handily placed seat offering great views.

3. Ignore bridleways to left and right and go ahead on the downhill bridleway that passes under power cables. *In the valley bottom a bridleway sign indicates that you should go ahead on an uphill, narrow, eroded and overgrown path at **point A** on my map.* Avoid this by forking right along the well-used track that later swings left alongside a field edge to meet a T-junction with a wide track.

Meeting a friendly dalmation in the woods.

4 Turn left along the track to soon meet a bridleway directional post. *The bridleway signed to the left points back to the overgrown path ignored in point 3*. Our route from here is to turn right on a wide downhill bridleway. Soon the track passes three remote cottages in the forest and you should continue ahead on their rough driveway until a country lane is reached.

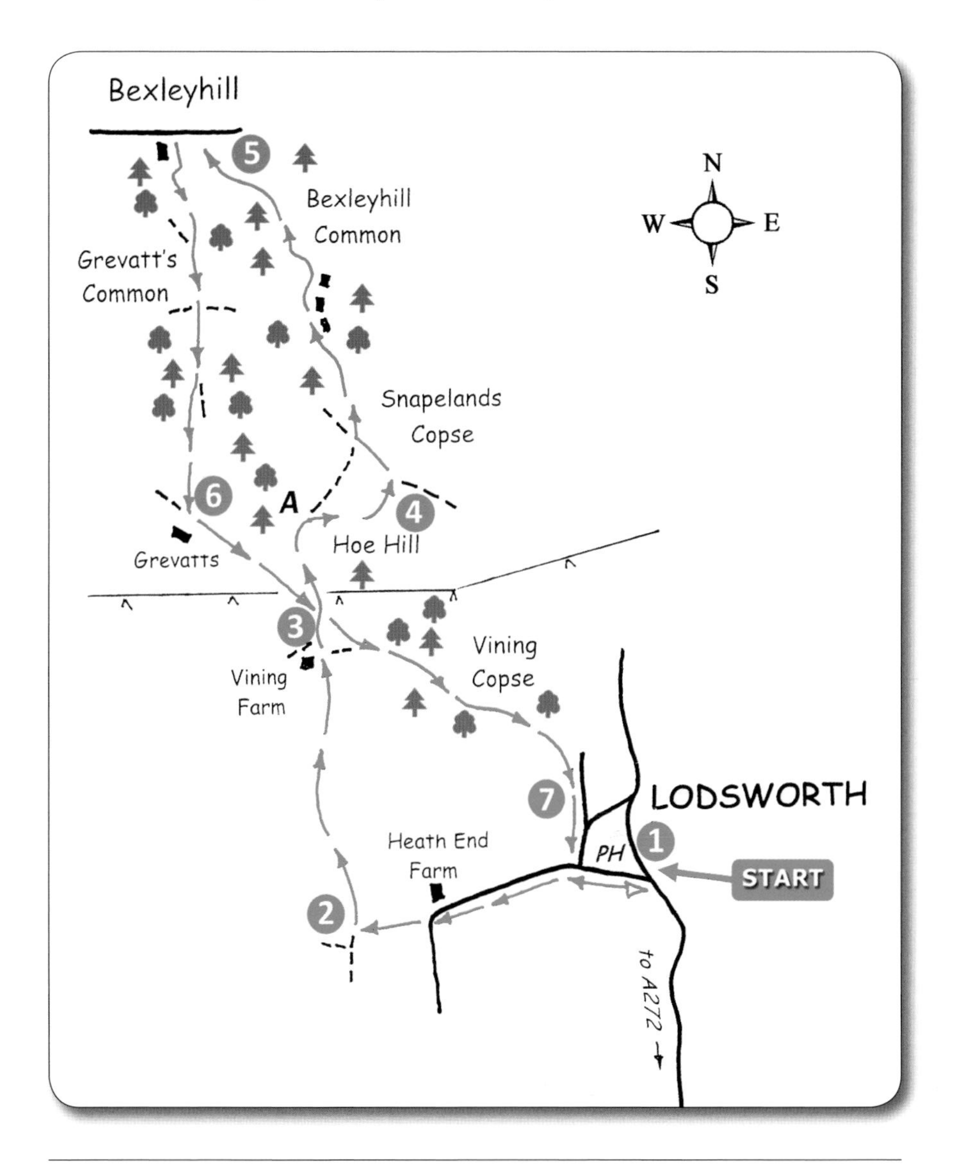

5. Turn left up the lane for 50 yards before turning left again on a signed footpath to the left of the driveway to **Nightingales**. The narrow path skirts the grounds and when at the rear of them, turns left up a deep gully. At the top of the gully a small grassy area is met alongside a directional post. Turn left here on a wide forestry track and soon go over a crossing track. Look out for a fork where the signed footpath follows the right fork.

6. The footpath ends at a T-junction with a cart track with **Grevatts barn** ahead and power cables beyond. The way turns left here along the track to soon rejoin the seat with views. Go ahead, pass the seat and paddock and at a larger track bear left along it until it ends at a road.

7. Maintain direction along the road and at a small road junction keep ahead. The road ends at a T-junction with **Gills Lane** where a left turn brings you back to the **Hollist Arms** to complete the figure-of-eight route.

A stunning view over the rural idyll as far as the South Downs in the distance.

8

Whiteways and Houghton Forest

The walk begins by the popular Whiteways Café.

This great walk for dogs and their companions has the lot: an easy-to-follow route along well-trodden paths and tracks, fantastic panoramic views from the top of the South Downs and shade from the summer sun as the way passes through Houghton Forest. Thankfully, some things are missing though, like stiles, cattle and roads. After leaving the popular picnic spot by Whiteways Café, the route climbs gently to meet the South Downs Way on top of Bury Hill. The way then follows the long distance path across the top of the downs to Westburton Hill where the only real climb of the circuit is encountered. Soon after passing the crest of Bignor Hill, the route turns and joins with the Monarch's Way long distance path, which descends easily through the peace and quiet of Houghton Forest to rejoin the car park and complete this wonderful circuit.

Terrain

Generally easy going apart from one short, sharp climb of 126 feet followed by an easier rise of 130 feet to reach the top of Bignor Hill – neither of which will trouble anyone of average fitness.

Where to park

Whiteways car park. **OS map:** Explorer 121 Arundel and Pulborough (GR: TQ 007 107).

How to get there

The car park is off Whiteways Lodge Roundabout 3 miles north of Arundel at the junction of the A284 and the A29.

Nearest refreshments

Whiteways Café in the car park offers a selection of hot and cold drinks and simple food. ☎ 01798 831892

The Walk

1. With your back to the road, follow a bridleway into woodland 80 yards to the right of **Whiteways Café**. In 200 yards turn right on another bridleway to soon meet a T-junction by an open field. Go left here and at the field end follow the path rightwards and continue along the field edge. The path climbs easily up **Bury Hill** and ends at a T-junction.

2. Turn left here along the well-signed **South Downs Way** long distance path. After a mile of expansive views a group of barns are met in a shallow valley. Pass the barns and 40 yards later follow the signed **South Downs Way** path

Dog factors

Distance: 5½ miles.
Road walking: None.
Livestock: None apart from maybe an occasional horse rider.
Stiles: None.
Nearest vets: Fitzalan House Veterinary Surgery, 2 Church Hill, Angmering BN16 4EG ☎ 01903 770437
(emergencies: 01903 713806)

left to meet a wide uphill track. Although quite steep, the hill is thankfully short and at its top ends at a T-junction.

3 Turn right and continue on the slowly rising track to meet the crest of **Bignor Hill** by **Toby's Stone**.

This unusual feature is a memorial to a former secretary of the local hunt in the form of horse-mounting steps.

Press on along the track to meet a small parking area and continue ahead to a finger-board at its end.

4 Leave the long distance path now by turning left on the path signed to **Slindon**. Soon, at a second finger-post by a junction of tracks, turn left again. This wide track is a section of the **Monarch's Way** long distance path. Ignore the occasional bridleway to left and right and keep to the long distance path – marked by small discs on the bridleway signposts.

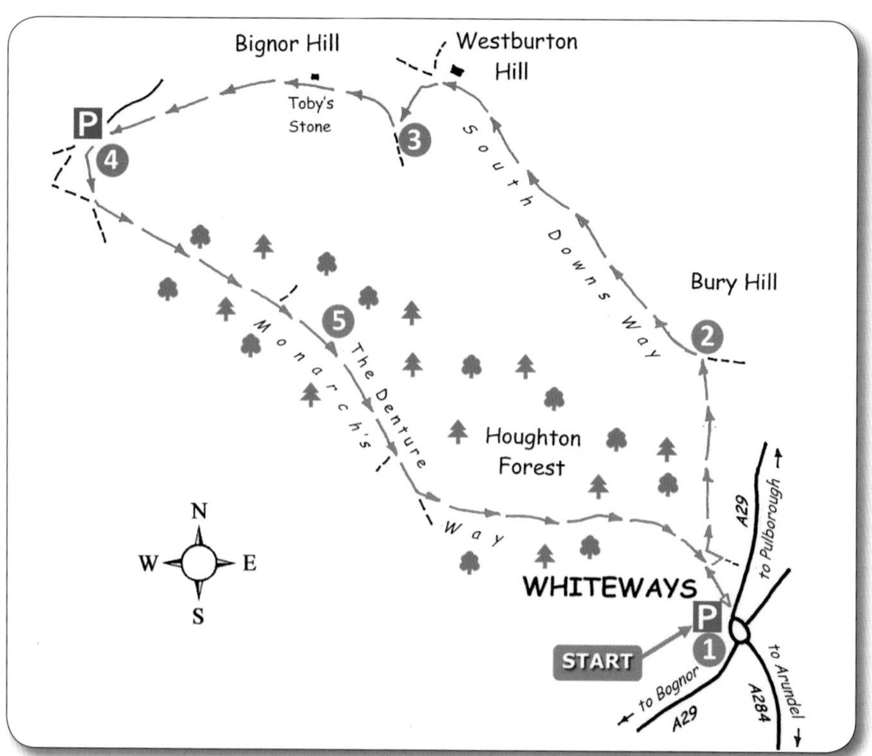

5 Along the way the track becomes known as **The Denture** and later forks left as it continues through **Houghton Forest**.

I have come across some odd place names before but 'The Denture' must take the dog biscuit. It is a corruption of the word Devonshire – a way of fertilising poor chalk soil by means of seasonal fire raising.

Keep ahead on the main track and ignore side paths until the car park and the end of this super walk are met.

The path across Bignor Hill offers wonderful views.

9

The Dover and Wepham Ball

Walking the dogs with a friend is always a pleasure.

The peace and tranquillity of this wonderful woodland walk around Angmering Park Estate is a real joy for dog walkers. The easily followed figure-of-eight route is along wide forestry tracks and drives that offer shade from the summer sun and, with only a small section ever likely to become muddy, makes for a great winter walk also. Dogs will enjoy the freedom of the entire route. Soon after leaving the car park the way goes through Lower Wepham Wood to meet its first turning point by Gibbet Piece. From here it turns east along a quiet estate drive to reach the next turning point and another wide forestry track. Heading south now, this lovely track through Lower Oldfield Copse brings you to the crossing point of your outward path and after continuing through more majestic woodland the way finally passes through Quakerscorner Copse and all too soon rejoins the car park.

Terrain

Fairly level.

Where to park

The car park in Butler's Copse. **OS map:** Explorer 121 Arundel and Pulborough (GR: TQ 060 065).

How to get there

The car park can only be reached from the east-bound lane of the A27, some 2½ miles east of the Littlehampton/Arundel roundabout. The turn-off is signed as Dover Lane and the car park is at the end of the lane.

Nearest refreshments

None along the route so why not take a picnic? Alternatively, in Arundel, next to the cathedral, is **St Mary's Gate Inn** where dogs are welcome in the bar or on the decking. It also has a car park. ☎ 01903 883145

The Walk

1. Go back to the car park entrance and turn right; pass through a gate to meet a junction of tracks in 50 yards. Go ahead on the track signed as a bridleway and when by a flint house follow it rightwards.

2. Pass a **Southern Water** facility to meet a junction of tracks in 120 yards. Here turn left through gates and ignore a track on your immediate left in 10 yards. Keep to this wonderful track through **Lower Wepham Wood** until it ends at a tarmac estate drive.

Dog factors

Distance: 3¾ miles.
Road walking: None although the occasional vehicle may be encountered as some of the way is along estate drives.
Livestock: None apart from the occasional horse rider.
Stiles: None.
Nearest vets: Fitzalan House Veterinary Surgery, 2 Church Hill, Angmering BN16 4EG ☎ 01903 770437
(emergencies: 01903 713806)

It was near this point back in 1774 that Jack Upperton's body was gibbeted after he was hanged for attempted robbery of the Royal Mail being carried on horseback by William Baldry. The gibbet is an iron cage containing the deceased person's body and was generally hung from the spot where the offence occurred. It prevented the relatives from recovering the deceased and, more importantly, acted as a warning to others.

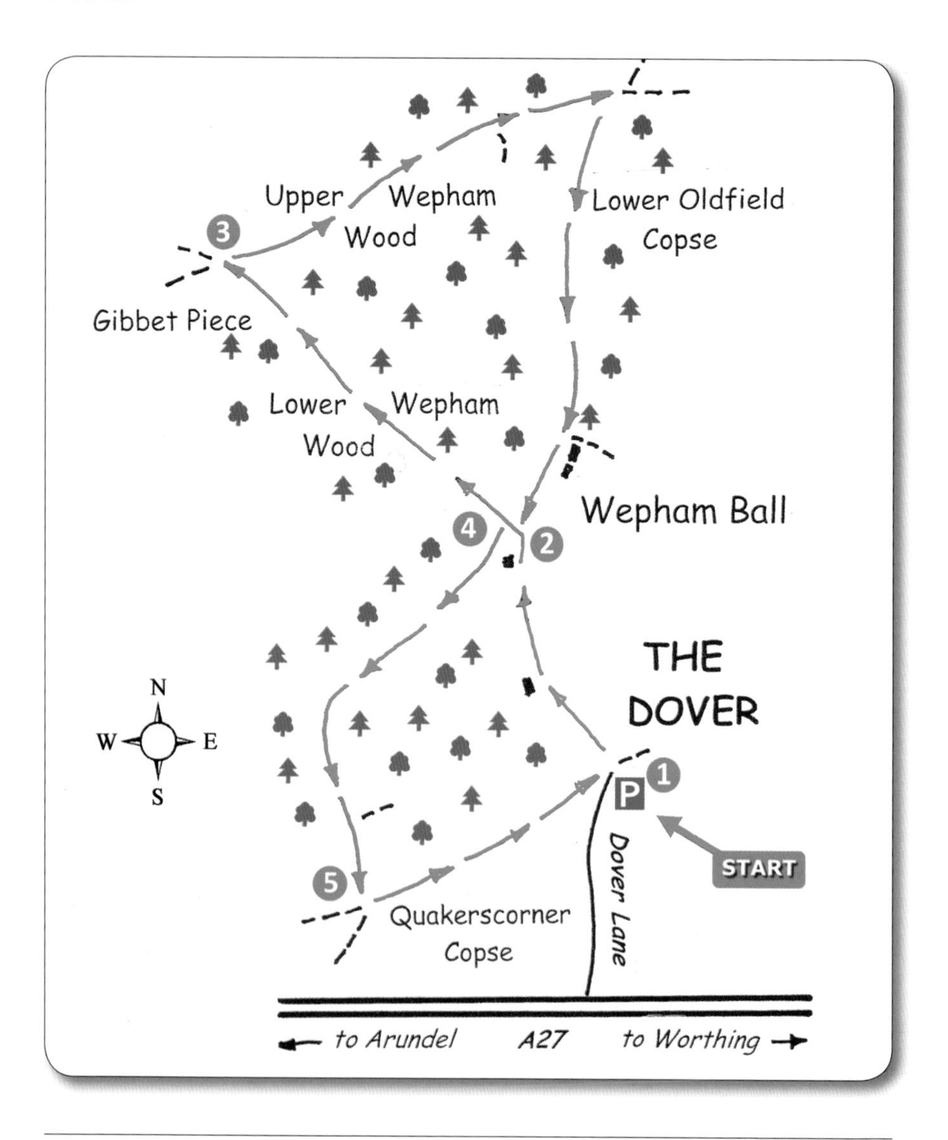

3 Turn right and continue along the drive until a stony track is met on your right at the foot of a dip. Turn right here and follow the track through **Lower Oldfield Copse**. Pass by cottages at **Wepham Ball** and ignore a signed footpath on your left. Soon you will rejoin your outward path at **point 2**.

The unusual name of Wepham Ball comes from the old English 'balle' – meaning a boundary beside a mound.

4 Here turn right through the gates you passed through earlier and in 10 yards go left on a signed footpath along a wide track. Later ignore a signed footpath on your left but 300 yards further on look out for a well-signed crossing bridleway.

5 Turn left here and follow the bridleway through **Quakerscorner Copse**. The bridleway brings you to an estate drive and after following it for a short distance a junction of tracks is met. Turn right here to reach the car park in 50 yards and the end of this enjoyable circuit.

Wide forestry tracks are a feature of this walk.

10

Loxwood and the Wey & Arun Canal

Flowers by the canal bank.

This not-to-be-missed walk is suitable for the young, old, big and small – and that's just the dogs! After beginning by the popular Onslow Arms pub, the circuit follows the pretty canal bank for almost 2 miles to reach the newly restored Drungewick Aqueduct. Turning away from the canal here along quiet Drungewick Lane, the route soon goes cross country and passes through the pretty bluebell wood of Birch Copse where the path follows a small woodland brook. After passing between well-fenced paddocks, the way brings you to an old watermill by a wonderful cluster of handsome houses, some dating back to the 17th century. Continuing on for a few more yards, the canal bank is soon rejoined for the short stroll back to the Onslow Arms and the end of this superb outing.

Terrain

Level.

Where to park

The public car park beyond the Onslow Arms' own parking. **OS map:** Explorer 134 Crawley and Horsham (GR: TQ 042 311).

How to get there

Loxwood and the Onslow Arms are on the B2133, south of Alfold and 4 miles north-west of Billingshurst. The Onslow Arms is at the southern end of the village.

Nearest refreshments

The **Onslow Arms** has a lovely dog-friendly garden and, as well as the usual pub fare, boasts of having the most delicious cakes and cream teas you have ever tasted! ☎ 01403 752452

The Walk

1. From the car park make your way to the canal bank and, with your back to the **Onslow Arms**, follow the well-trodden path alongside the pretty canal. Soon pass by a set of lock gates to reach a quiet country lane. Cross the lane, pass through a gate opposite and continue alongside the canal.

Dog factors

Distance: 3½ miles.
Road walking: ¼ mile of quiet lane without pavements; 1 country lane to cross.
Livestock: None, although you may meet the occasional horse rider.
Stiles: None.
Nearest vets: Pet Doctors Veterinary Clinic, 3 Jengers Mead, Billingshurst RH14 9PB ☎ 01403 783444

❷ Along the way pass **Baldwin's Knob Lock** and later the restored **Drungewick Aqueduct** to meet **Drungewick Lane** where the path ends.

The Wey and Arun Canal opened in 1816 and formed the link between two waterways; the river Arun at Pallingham in Sussex, and the Wey Navigation at Shalford, Surrey. As the canal passed through a mainly rural landscape, it never carried enough freight to make it a commercial success and so was abandoned 55 years later. Stalwarts of The Wey & Arun Canal Trust began their restoration efforts in 1970 and this wonderful section of the walk follows the fruits of their early labours. They aim to bring the canal back to navigation and provide a waterway link from London to Littlehampton, via the rivers Wey and Arun.

❸ Turn right along the quiet lane, passing by **Drungewick Manor**. Just 40 yards before meeting the sign for **Bumble Farm**, turn right on a well-signed bridleway and pass between a house and a paddock before pressing on ahead on a grassy track through trees. When a cart track enters from the left, go ahead to meet a bridleway sign and fork left as directed.

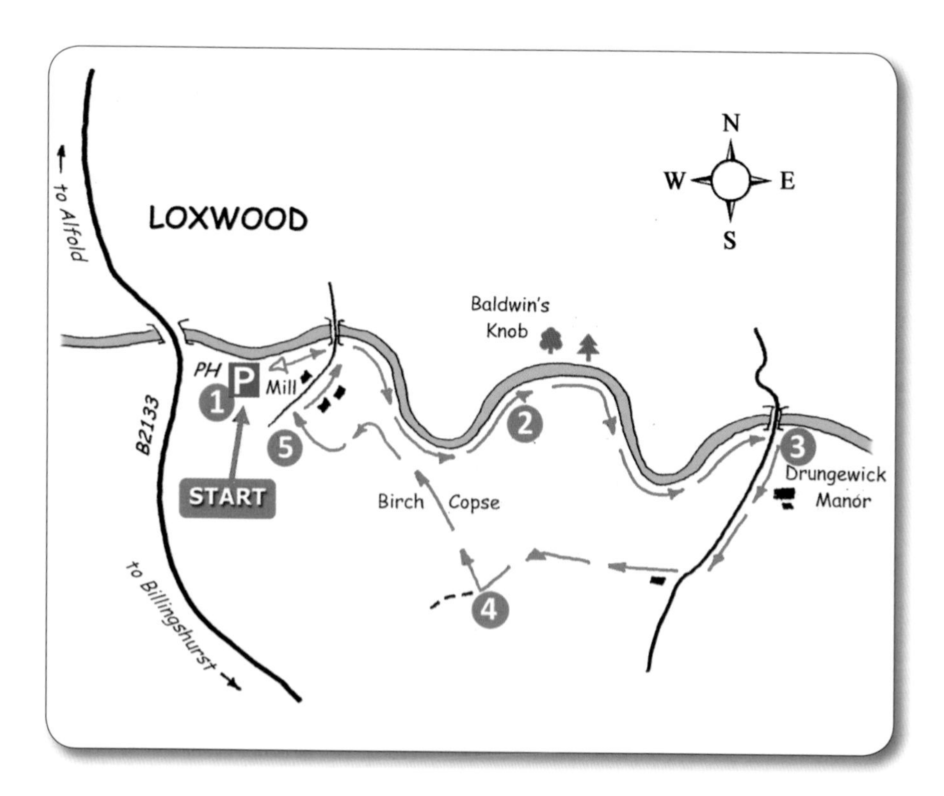

4 After rounding a shallow right bend, look out for a footpath sign on your left directing you rightwards. Follow this footpath as it leads you through **Birch Copse** and alongside a woodland brook. As you exit the woodland, pass through a gate and continue on a fenced path that soon zigzags between paddocks.

5 At the path end, go through a gate to meet a concrete drive. Go right along the drive to meet a T-junction with a quiet lane. Turn right along the lane to soon pass between an old watermill and a wonderful cluster of ancient houses. Press on a little further and the canal bank is reached where a left turn soon brings you to the end of this lovely walk.

Enjoying a shady path through the trees.

11

The Mens and Hammonds Wood

Easy walking through Hammonds Wood.

This wonderful woodland circuit leads you through the wild and largely unmanaged forest of The Mens, a Site of Special Scientific Interest looked after by the Sussex Wildlife Trust. The route is easy to follow and gives dogs the freedom to roam at will between the trees in this beautiful and ancient woodland. After circling Crimbourne House and Stud Farm, the way heads south on a well-marked footpath to reach its farthest point at the tiny hamlet of Bedham. From here the route returns along a wide bridleway through the forest and later passes through Hawkhurst Court. The four seasons at The Mens are represented by springtime wildflowers, cool shade from the summer sun, interesting autumnal fungi and winter mud! So, winter here is best avoided, but it's a great walk for the rest of the year. Oh, and if you are wondering about the name, The Mens is a corruption of an Anglo-Saxon word 'ge-maennes', meaning common land.

Terrain

Undulating with one steady rise of 200 feet.

Where to park

Sussex Wildlife Trust car park at The Mens. **OS map:** Explorer 134 Crawley and Horsham (GR: TQ 023 236).

How to get there

Turn south off the A272 at a minor crossroads on a lane signed to Crimbourne, 3½ miles west of Wisborough Green and 3½ miles east of Petworth. The car park is on your right in 150 yards.

Nearest refreshments

None along the route so you could try the cosy **Cricketers Arms** pub in Durbans Road, Wisborough Green, where dogs are welcome in the bar area. It also has a sunny outside seating area to the front overlooking the village green. As you sit and relax after your walk, you can watch the energetic residents of Wisborough Green play cricket, football or the 15th-century traditional Sussex game of stoolbar, all of which take place on the village green. ☎ 01403 700369

The Walk

1 From the car park entrance go diagonally right across the road to meet and follow a well-worn path through the trees. Soon, with a ditch and bank on

Dog factors

Distance: 4 miles.
Road walking: ½ mile of quiet country lane and 2 lanes to cross.
Livestock: None but maybe an occasional horse rider as there are bridleways in The Mens.
Stiles: None.
Nearest vets: Newbridge Veterinary Surgery, Wharf Farm (on the A272), Wisborough Green RH14 0JG ☎ 01403 784777

your right, follow the path leftwards and, after crossing a small bridge over a brook, the path ends at a T-junction with a wide track.

2 Turn right along the track, passing **West Cottage**, to reach the gate of **Freelands**. Here go right for 10 yards before continuing along the signed bridleway through woodland. After crossing a footbridge, follow the bridleway right, ignoring a footpath signed on your left. The bridleway ends at a small lane.

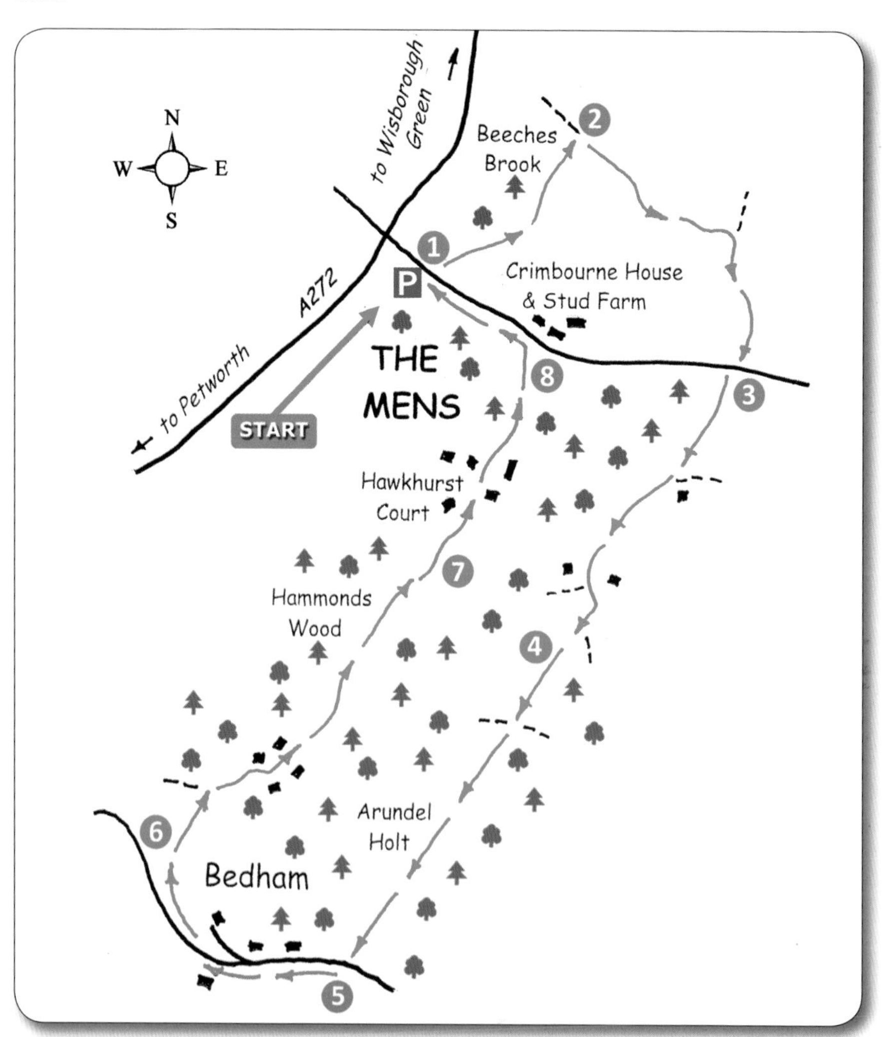

3 Go right along the lane for 25 yards before turning left on a signed footpath through the forest. Ignore a crossing path and press on ahead to meet a drive. Go right along the drive. When a house named **Oaklees** is met, fork left along the drive and just after passing the gateway of **The Squirrels** follow the signed path rightwards alongside a garden. Go downhill and cross a bridge over a woodland brook. Here ignore paths signed to left and right and press on ahead out of the dell to meet a paddock fence.

4 The path follows the side of the paddock before continuing through the forest. Keep to the straight path as it begins to climb and ignore all crossing paths and tracks. The path ends at a country lane.

5 Turn right along the lane. Ignore a right fork and continue on the lane until opposite the gate to **Manor Farm**. Here fork right on a downhill bridleway where you will soon discover a ruin between the trees.

The ruin is of a small elementary school built in 1880. The single room was divided by a curtain to provide classrooms for both infants and seniors. At the end of school on a Friday, the curtain was withdrawn, the desks turned east and the building

A surprise find in the forest.

became a church. The school closed in 1925 but fortnightly church services continued for some time. The last recorded use of the building was in 1959 when it was used for a wedding.

6 The bridleway continues downhill between banks to meet a T-junction. Turn right here and soon cross a track to meet a second track. Continue left along this track and, just after passing **The Orchards**, follow the signed bridleway leftwards. Keep to the marked bridleway through woodland and at an indistinct fork, keep left on the bridleway.

7 The bridleway brings you to a drive which you should follow leftwards. The drive leads you through a wonderful cluster of fine houses in **Hawkhurst Court**.

Hawkhurst Court was a country house used by the Canadian Army during the Second World War and was where the Dieppe Raid was planned in 1942. It later became a private school before converting to housing during the 1980s.

8 Follow the drive to meet **Crimbourne Lane** opposite the grounds of **Crimbourne House and Stud Farm**. Turn left along the lane to reach the car park and the end of this super walk in ¼ mile.

Kithurst Hill and Amberley Mount

The view across Wepham Down.

The outstanding scenery and easy-to-follow paths and tracks make this great circuit, the longest in this book, a must. The route leaves the top of Kithurst Hill by crossing arable fields with panoramic views before passing through well-kept Lee Farm. Turning west here, the way continues along dog-friendly wide tracks, lined with wildflowers in early summer, as it crosses rolling Wepham Down. The views along the whole route are far-reaching and the peace and tranquillity of the setting are a delight. The circuit then begins to head to the top of the downs on a fairly steady climb to meet Amberley Mount and join with the popular South Downs Way long distance path, which it follows along the top of the downs for the last two miles.

Terrain

Undulating with one steady rise of 330 feet that should not trouble anyone of average fitness.

Where to park

Kithurst Hill car park. **OS map:** Explorer 121 Arundel and Pulborough (GR: TQ 070 124).

How to get there

Take the B2139 and the car park is signed to the south, 2 miles east of Amberley and just over 1 mile west of Storrington. Follow the single track lane to the top of the downs to meet the car park.

Nearest refreshments

There are plenty of picnic spots, with wonderful views, along the route or you could call in at the dog-friendly **Anchor Inn**, High Street, Storrington for a good selection of bar food. Your dog is more than welcome in the shade of the bar or you can all sun yourselves at a table in the garden. ☎ 01903 742665.

The Walk

❶ Go to the car park entrance, turn right and pass gates to reach the **South Downs Way** long distance path. Turn right here for 20 yards before turning left through a pedestrian gate to enter a large arable field. Follow a well-trodden path across the centre of the field to meet a hedgerow and crossing bridleway. Keep ahead here and pass through the next field.

Dog factors

Distance: 6¾ miles.
Road walking: None.
Livestock: The route passes through one sheep pasture (see point 5) plus you may meet the occasional horse rider.
Stiles: None.
Nearest vets: Crossways Veterinary Group, 43 School Hill, Storrington RH20 4NA ☎ 01903 743040

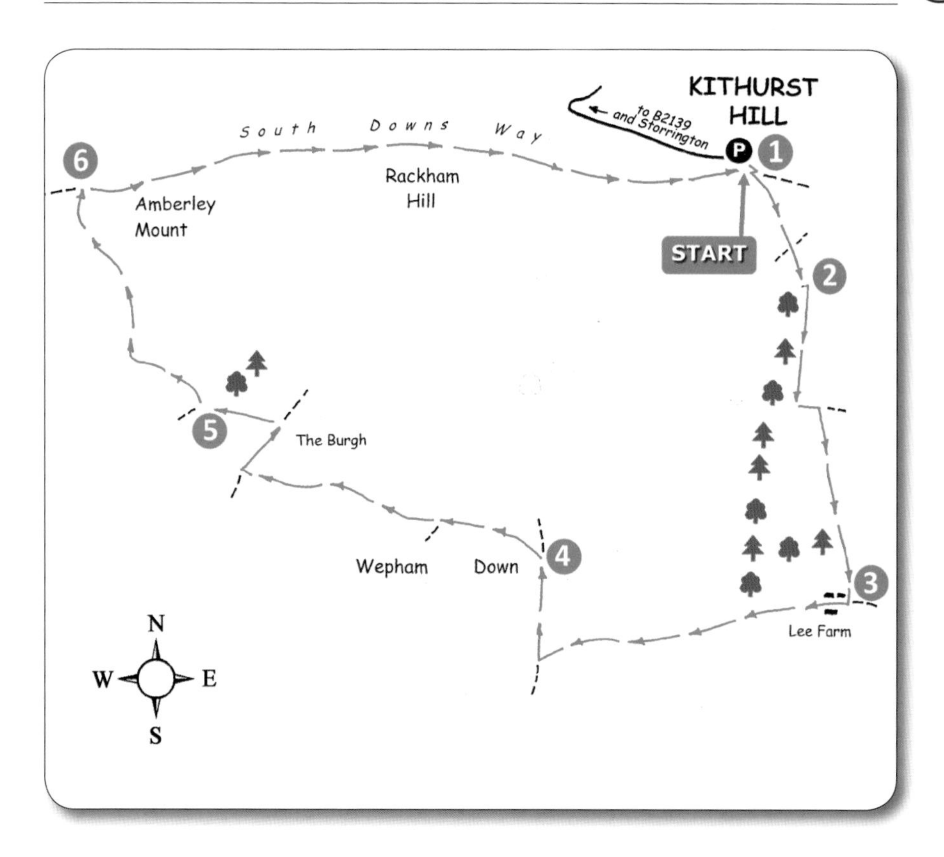

2 At the field end, enter woodland and turn left as directed before turning right in 25 yards on a path alongside a ribbon of woodland. Later ignore a bridleway on your right and continue ahead to the field end. Here follow the field edge leftwards and soon, on a dip slope, turn right on a wide farm track that ends at **Lee Farm**.

3 Turn right now on the wide track and pass between farm buildings. Remain on this lovely track for 1 mile until it meets a junction of tracks. Here turn right, pass by a gate and go ahead along a cart track. Pass by a second gate to reach a bend in the track before a third gate.

4 Follow the cart track left and remain on it as it crosses undulating scenery for 1 mile to end at a T-junction. Now turn right along a cart track until it is met by another on the left. Here turn left and on a downward slope after rounding a shallow left bend look out for a directional post on your left.

5 Here turn right on the signed bridleway and soon pass through a pedestrian gate to enter a sheep pasture. Follow a grassy cart track to the valley floor where you should ignore a gate ahead of you in the distance and immediately turn right. Go through a gate in the field edge and follow a rising path. After passing along the left side of rising fields, press on ahead to reach the **South Downs Way** long distance footpath.

6 Turn right along the well-signed path as it climbs **Amberley Mount** and take in the superb views over **Amberley** with the **river Arun** beyond. From here the way is well-signed and little more than gently undulating for the remaining 2 miles to the car park.

On the path across Rackham Hill.

Findon Valley and Cissbury Ring

Paddy enjoying playing in the fields.

This excellent dog walk passes through the wonderful scenery of Findon Valley and, towards its end, takes in a slice of English history. For almost the entire route dogs have the freedom to roam and explore to their hearts' content. After leaving the outskirts of Worthing, the route passes to the north of Cissbury Ring as it heads for the Monarch's Way long distance path, which it follows for a while. After turning and continuing through Stump Bottom and Canada Bottom, the way begins a fairly easy climb to reach the Iron Age fortifications of Cissbury Ring. Here the route continues through the centre of the fort to meet and follow the western ramparts before finally going downhill over open fields to complete this stunning circuit.

Terrain

Undulating, with one none-too-difficult rise of 230 feet that should not trouble anyone of average fitness.

Where to park

Storrington Rise car park. **OS map:** Explorer 121 Arundel and Pulborough (GR: TQ 128 077).

How to get there

From the A24 the car park is signed as Cissbury Ring, 1¼ miles north of the A27/A24 roundabout in Worthing. From the north, follow the A24 for 1 mile beyond the Findon bypass roundabout to see the car park sign. Drive along May Tree Avenue for a few yards before turning left into Storrington Rise to reach the car park.

Nearest refreshments

None on the route but there are many superb picnic spots around Cissbury Ring. One mile away in The Square at Findon is the dog-friendly **Village House Hotel**, which serves a good selection of food. Dogs are most welcome in the bar area and of course in the sunny garden. ☎ 01903 873350

Dog factors

Distance: 5½ miles.
Road walking: None.
Livestock: 1 field at point 2 contains livestock at times plus you may meet the occasional horse rider.
Stiles: None.
Nearest vets: Northdale Veterinary Practice, 162 Findon Road, Findon Valley BN14 0EL
☎ 01903 265968

The Walk

1 From the centre of the left side of the car park, go between posts and cross a grassy area diagonally right to meet a well-trodden path. Follow the rising path along the left side of a large grassy area with a hedgerow to your left. At the top of the open space, fork leftwards on a bridleway through woodland.

2 Pass through a gate across the path, where it is requested that dogs should be on leads. Press on through the field with splendid views over the valley and exit via a second gate. Go ahead to meet a directional post.

3 Go left here; ignore a drive on your left and a track to your right. The route is ahead on a slowly rising stony track. At the top of the rise, just before the track

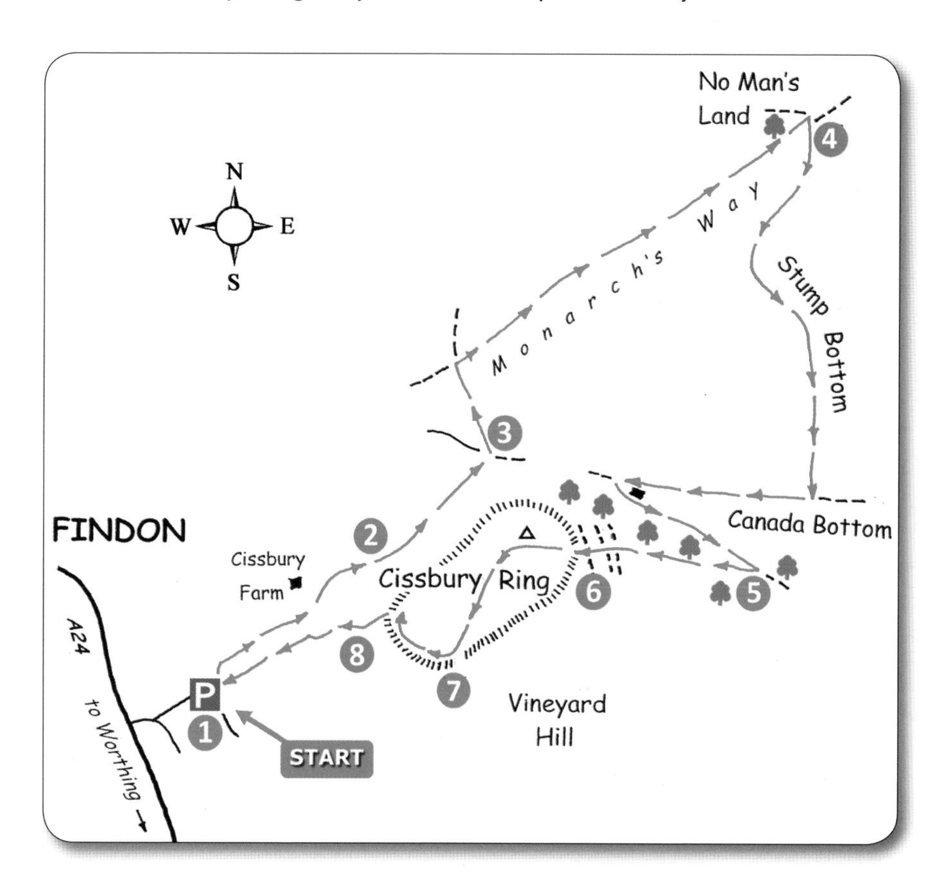

widens, a directional post is met where the **Monarch's Way** long distance path crosses the track. Turn right here and follow the narrow long distance path for 1 mile alongside fenced fields until a stony track is reached.

4 Turn right for 20 yards and ignore the **Monarch's Way** to your left. The route is ahead on a bridleway between fenced fields. Soon pass through a pedestrian gate and continue on the path that leads you easily through **Stump Bottom**. The path ends at a T-junction with a wide track in **Canada Bottom** beside restored **Lychpole Dewpond**. Turn right along the track and 60 yards after passing a large barn, turn left through a **National Trust** gate on a bridleway.

5 Just before a second **National Trust** gate turn right, almost back on yourself, and follow a narrow, uphill chalky path. As you near the top of the climb, ignore a crossing path and another in 25 yards and keep ahead to reach a bridleway marker post at a third crossing track.

The path through Stump Bottom.

6 Here, go ahead through a kissing gate and pass through a breach in the defensive bank of **Cissbury Ring**. Press on ahead and ignore a left fork in 25 yards. Pass the **triangulation point** and continue ahead. Follow the wide grassy path as it bends left and passes through a tree line to reach another breach in the defensive bank.

Cissbury Ring is the second largest hill fort in England and dates from around 250 BC. The breach you passed through earlier and the one you are now facing are of a much later date. During the Second World War the 2nd Argyll and Sutherland Highlanders were stationed here and the breaches were made to accommodate the passage of large guns to fire at enemy ships in the English Channel.

7 Climb steps to the right of the breach and follow the top of the defensive bank for just over ¼ mile to reach a set of concrete steps that allow you to descend to, and pass through, a kissing gate with a **memorial seat** to its left. There are two grassy downhill paths ahead; either brings you to a second kissing gate in the right corner of this open space.

8 Go through the kissing gate; turn right through a ribbon of trees, taking care not to trip on the exposed roots, and come to a large, grassy open space. Now go downhill to reach the car park in the distance and the end of this exhilarating walk.

Wiston and Chanctonbury Ring

A fine summer's day on the South Downs Way.

This is a cracking circuit that both two-legged and four-legged friends will enjoy. Beginning below the north flank of the South Downs, the route follows mainly wide tracks and bridleways eastwards before turning and climbing to the top of the downs. Take your time as the rise is fairly stiff, but well worthwhile as the rewards are great: 360° breath-taking views of the surrounding countryside. After joining the South Downs Way long distance path the route passes by the ancient hill fort of Chanctonbury Ring. This is what the newly formed South Downs National Park is all about

– great walking and lovely countryside for all to enjoy. After descending from these heights, the route follows more wide tracks through lovely woodland to bring you to the car park and the end of this invigorating walk. Chanctonbury Ring takes its name from the ring of trees on the site of a small hill fort on top of Chanctonbury Hill. Pottery fragments and carbon dating of animal bones suggest the site was used from the early Iron Age to the Bronze Age. The Romans also appreciated the location. They built two temples here for religious ceremonies. The beech trees were originally planted in the 1760s, but were blown down in the Great Storm of 1987. They have since been replanted and the site restored to its former glory. From the top there are commanding views across the weald. This is a popular spot with dog walkers so there will be plenty of opportunities for your hound to find some four legged friends to meet and greet.

Terrain

One rise of 480 feet to the top of the downs that should not trouble anyone of average fitness; other than that, gently undulating or downhill.

Where to park

Chanctonbury Ring car park. **OS map:** Explorer 121 Arundel and Pulborough (GR: TQ 146 124)

How to get there

From the A283 between Storrington and Bramber, the car park is signed southwards, 1½ miles east of the A283/A24 roundabout by the village of Washington. Follow the single track lane for ¾ mile to meet the car park on your left.

Nearest refreshments

Picnic on the heights of Chanctonbury Ring or, alternatively, tea, coffee, real ales and all the usual lunchtime bites are available at the **Frankland Arms** in Washington village where well-behaved dogs on leads can join you in the bar or sleep off the walk in the garden. ☎ 01903 892220

The Walk

1. From the car park entrance, go left along the lane to soon reach a junction of tracks by **Malthouse Cottage**. Turn left on a signed footpath along a stony track and pass between the buildings of **Great Barn Farm**. The farmer requests that dogs be kept on leads here as there is livestock, albeit in well-fenced fields. Press on and maintain direction along a shady cart track.

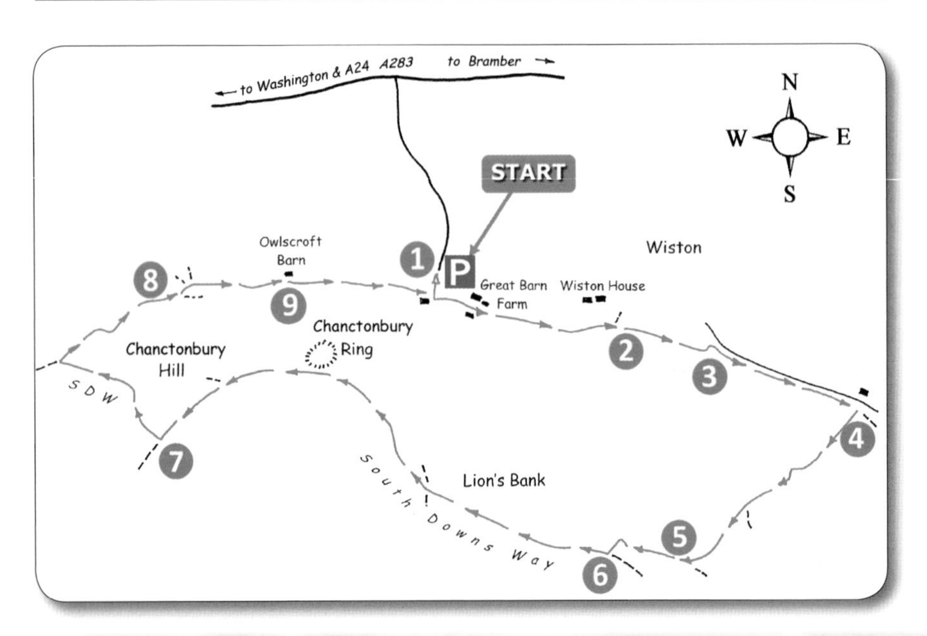
to Washington & A24
A283
to Bramber
N
W
E
S
START
Owlscroft Barn
Wiston
Great Barn Farm
Wiston House
Chanctonbury Ring
Chanctonbury Hill
SDW
Lion's Bank
South Downs Way
1
2
3
4
5
6
7
8
9
P

Dog factors

Distance: 6¼ miles.
Road walking: 150 yards of quiet country lane.
Livestock: Fenced off livestock for ¼ mile, sheep on open downland for ¼ mile (see point 6) and maybe the occasional horse rider.
Stiles: 4, easy for all but the very largest dogs.
Nearest vets: Crossways Veterinary Group, 2 High Street, Steyning BN44 3GG
☎ 01903 816428

The route passes close to Chanctonbury Ring.

2 Pass under an ornate footbridge and 90 yards later the track bends left. Here, fork right on a stony footpath and maintain direction. Soon the path becomes grassy with views of the downs on your right. Cross a stile and follow the path rightwards before it soon swings left to another stile.

3 Cross the stile and pass through a strip of woodland to reach an open field. Turn left along the field edge and soon follow it rightwards. Keep to the field edge as it remains parallel to a country lane on the other side of the hedgerow.

4 At the field end, go down steps to meet a crossing bridleway. Turn right on the bridleway, which later narrows and brings you to woodland. Go ahead along a broad track between trees for 35 yards before forking left on the signed bridleway. At a second directional post, go left and ignore a kissing gate to your left. Keep to this uphill bridleway as it climbs to the top of the downs.

5 When the bridleway exits woodland it is met by another from the left; go right. The narrow path follows a fenced field and, after swinging left, ends at the **South Downs Way** long distance path.

6 Turn right now along the well-signed **South Downs Way**, which offers superb panoramic views over the landscape and as far as the sea. As you near **Chanctonbury Ring**, go through a gate beside a cattle grid, which indicates that sheep graze this hilltop. Pass the ancient hill fort and go by a second cattle grid, leaving the sheep behind.

7 At a fork in the track, follow the long distance path right, where it soon begins its descent on a chalky track lined by orchids during early summer. When the track begins to level and with a field to your right, look out for a directional post opposite a pedestrian gate on your right. Turn sharp right here through the field, going almost back on yourself, to reach another gate at the edge of woodland.

8 Follow a wide, shady track and at a fork by tall pine trees with a field to your left, keep left. Soon follow the track leftwards to meet a junction of paths in 50 yards by field gates. Turn right through a gate and continue on a bridleway alongside woodland. Along the way pass tumbledown **Owlscroft Barn**.

9 Press on ahead on a footpath that runs alongside a forestry track and maintain direction to reach **Malthouse Cottage**. Turn left here to soon rejoin the car park to bring this wonderful circuit to an end.

Copsale and Southwater Country Park

Southwater Country Park is a peaceful spot for walkers.

This easy-to-follow walk is suitable for any time of the year and is especially good during winter or after heavy rain as much of it is along hard-surfaced paths and drives. Beginning at Copsale, this pan-handle shaped route follows the Downs Link long distance path, which offers you easy walking and your dog plenty of freedom away from roads, to reach Southwater Country Park, where it turns and passes the Visitor Centre, café and scenic lake. This is a lovely place to stop and watch the waterfowl or even picnic awhile at the water's edge. After leaving the Country Park, the route passes housing and continues through Blinks Wood to reach a quiet driveway as it begins to head back to rejoin the long distance path on the outskirts of Southwater. The route once again passes the Country Park from where it is a level stroll back to Copsale.

Terrain

One small hill, otherwise level.

Where to park

The small car park beside the Downs Link path in Copsale. **OS map:** Explorer 134 Crawley and Horsham (GR: TQ 171 248).

How to get there

Copsale is south-east of Southwater and signed from the A24 south of Southwater. If travelling north on the A24, Copsale is signed 800 yards north of its junction with the A272. Follow the signed road for 1 mile to meet the car park on your right.

Nearest refreshments

Southwater Country Park Café offers a good choice of simple fare at lunchtime and is open every day throughout the year, apart from at Christmas. Dogs will enjoy sitting with you at one of the many outdoor tables overlooking the lake. ☎ 01403 734607

Dog factors

Distance: 4¼ miles.
Road walking: ¼ mile of residential road with pavements, 250 yards of country lane with narrow verge and ½ mile of driveway without pavements; 4 easy road crossings.
Livestock: At point 5 there is a small field that occasionally has cows in it. NB: dogs must be on leads in Southwater Country Park between April and September.
Stiles: 1 (see point 4), easy for all but the very largest of dogs.
Nearest vets: Downs Link Veterinary Surgery, 16 Lintot Square, Fairbank Road, Southwater RH13 9LA.
☎ 01403 732219

The Walk

1 With the car park entrance at your back, go diagonally left across the road to meet the **Downs Link** long distance path. Turn right and continue along it. After passing a gate, the path forks left and goes under the busy **A24** main road. Keep to the signed path and later cross a quiet road to reach the entranceway of **Southwater Country Park**.

2 Turn left; enter the **Country Park** and soon fork right to meet the water's edge. Turn left now on a path alongside the water and pass the **Visitor Centre** and **café**.

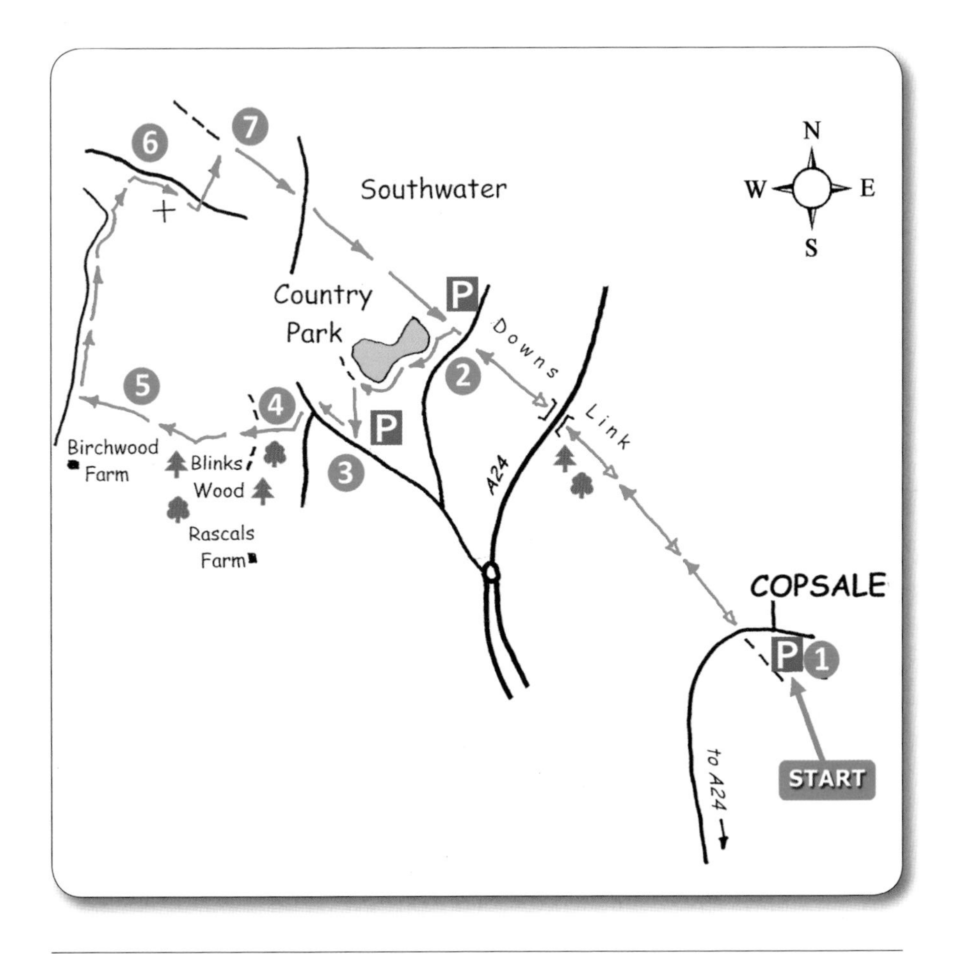

To protect the local wildlife, dogs must be on leads between April and September whilst walking in Southwater Country Park. The 90 acre park was formed during the early 1980s from the site of a redundant brickworks.

Keep to this path, which remains close to the lake. After rounding a right bend and crossing a small wooden bridge, turn left on a stony uphill path to reach a couple of seats. Here go left to soon pass by a gate and come to a small car park.

Ready for a day's walking.

3 Go out to the road and turn right alongside it until **Shipley Road** is met on your left. Turn left along it for 50 yards before turning right on a signed footpath between bungalows. Pass through a kissing gate and press on through peaceful **Blinks Wood**.

4 In 130 yards ignore a crossing path but 30 yards later, fork right on the signed footpath. Keep to the main path and look out for a footpath sign directing you leftwards. Go left to meet a stile beside a gate in 40 yards where you should turn right and press on along a fenced path beside a field. Pass through a second gate and ignore a path on your right. Keep ahead and cross a footbridge over a woodland brook.

5 At a field, pass through a gate and continue ahead along its edge to soon meet a concrete drive. Turn right along the drive and remain on it until it bends left. Here, continue ahead over a stile and enter an arable field. Press on ahead through the centre of the field to meet a lane.

6 Turn right along the lane; pass **Vicarage Cottage** and the **Church of the Holy Innocents** and look out for a signed bridleway on your left along the concrete drive to **College Farm**. Go left here to soon meet the **Downs Link** path, which crosses the drive.

7 Turn right along the well-signed path, which soon enters **Southwater** and crosses a road via pedestrian lights. Pass the **Village Surgery** and continue along the **Downs Link** path, passing **Southwater Country Park**. Now, with no need for further instruction, continue along the long distance path until you reach the end of this good walk in **Copsale**.

Bramber and the river Adur

The river Adur at Upper Beeding.

This varied and stimulating village, downland and riverside walk is superb exercise for man and beast alike. Beginning in the centre of Bramber, the circuit follows pretty village streets lined with ancient houses. After passing through Upper Beeding the route sets out for the heights of the South Downs on a fairly stiff climb that should not trouble a person of average fitness and certainly not our four-legged friends. The effort expended is well rewarded when the open downs are reached where dogs can run freely; savour the fantastic views as the South Downs stretch away far into the distance, or even picnic awhile at this glorious spot. After making the easy descent along the South Downs Way path, the route meets the bank of the meandering river Adur where there is every chance of seeing interesting wildlife; I spotted a little egret last time I passed this way. The route now follows the river bank for the last mile to rejoin the village street, from where it is just a short stroll to complete this charming walk.

Terrain

One steep hill with the remainder of the circuit either downhill or level.

Where to park

The car park in the centre of Bramber. **OS map:** Explorer 122 Brighton and Hove (GR: TQ 187 106).

How to get there

Bramber is reached via the A283. Turn off eastwards 3 miles north of the A27 at Shoreham.

Nearest refreshments

The **Castle Inn** opposite the car park. Dogs on leads are welcome in the bar area and garden (not the restaurant) and should you wish to stay, there is even a dog-friendly bedroom. The inn offers a good selection of lunchtime bites. ☎ 01903 812102

Dog factors

Distance: 3½ miles.
Road walking: 1 mile of village streets with pavements; 2 busy road crossings (see points 2 and 4).
Livestock: None, although you may meet the occasional horse rider.
Stiles: 2, both dog-friendly.
Nearest vets: Crossways Veterinary Group, 2 High Street, Steyning BN44 3GG ☎ 01903 816428

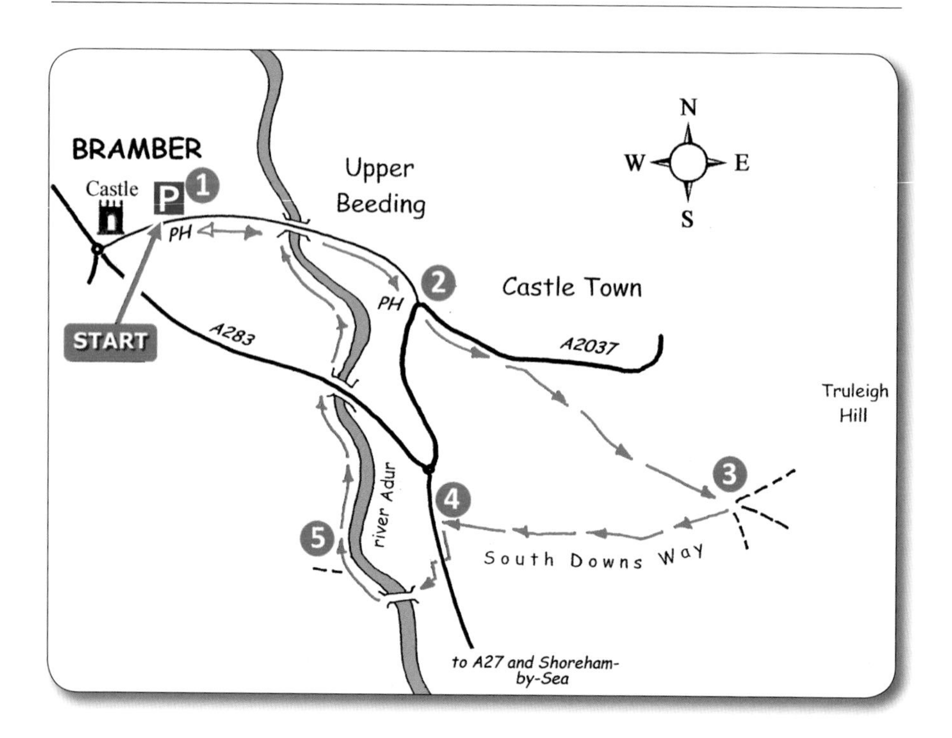

The Walk

❶ Cross the road from the car park and turn left along the pavement, passing the **Castle Inn**. Continue on the pavement as you walk along the pretty village street and cross the **river Adur** as you enter **Upper Beeding**. Follow the road rightwards at a small roundabout to reach the **Rising Sun** public house.

❷ Cross the road leftwards here and continue along **Henfield Road** until you meet a stony private drive on your right named **The Bostal**, signed as a bridleway. Follow this uphill track, which leads you to the top of the downs.

❸ The bridleway ends at a small stony parking area and our way is now rightwards through a gate where a magnificent panorama opens up across the **Adur Valley** and **Bramber** – savour the views as you get your breath back. The way continues on a grassy path, which begins to descend into the **Adur Valley**. Although this is sheep country, they are well-fenced and dogs will enjoy the freedom the downland offers.

4 Finally the path ends at the busy **A283**. Turn left alongside the road to reach a car parking area opposite. Cross the road with caution and seek out a well-trodden path signed as the **South Downs Way**. Follow the path as it passes a horse trough and water tap to reach and cross a bridge over the **river Adur**.

5 Turn right at the far side of the bridge and when the hard-surfaced path bends left, press on alongside the river. Keep to the peaceful river bank as it passes under the **A283** road and finally brings you to **Upper Beeding Bridge** where a left turn along the village street returns you to the car park.

A quiet shady spot for you to have a quick rest while your dog can lap up some water from the drinking trough.

Mannings Heath and St Leonard's Forest

Space to stretch your legs!

This lovely route around St Leonard's Forest is just perfect for dogs of all sizes. With acres of space among the trees to explore and wide tracks to race up and down; it's a dog's paradise. The solitude of the majestic forest where birdsong resounds from the treetops, the scent of pine hanging on the breeze and the ease of the route are a total joy for dog walkers, and there are plenty of woodland picnic spots to choose from. A section of the walk follows a mile-long track known as Mick Mills' Race where folklore dictates that the said person was a smuggler who was told that the Devil had come to collect his soul. A deal was struck that involved racing the Devil through the forest with the winner claiming Mick's soul. Mick won – an unlikely story I would say!

Terrain

Fairly level.

Where to park

Roosthole Forestry Commission car park. **OS map:** Explorer 134 Crawley and Horsham (GR: TQ 208 298).

How to get there

Mannings Heath is on the A281 between Cowfold and Horsham. At the southern end of the village follow Church Road, signed to Mannings Heath Golf Club. When the road finally ends at a T-junction, turn left to reach the car park in 250 yards on your right.

Nearest refreshments

The **Dun Horse Inn** on the A281 north of Church Road is a dog-friendly pub serving a good selection of real ales and well prepared food. The large enclosed garden is ideal for an al fresco lunch. ☎ 01403 265783

The Walk

1. Leave the car park by passing a low-vehicle barrier and following a wide, slowly rising hard surfaced track between the trees. Continue until it ends at a T-junction.

Dog factors

Distance: 3½ miles.
Road walking: None.
Livestock: None, although you may meet the occasional horse rider.
Stiles: None.
Nearest vets: Arthur Lodge Veterinary Surgery, 17 Brighton Road, Horsham RH13 5BE ☎ 01403 252964

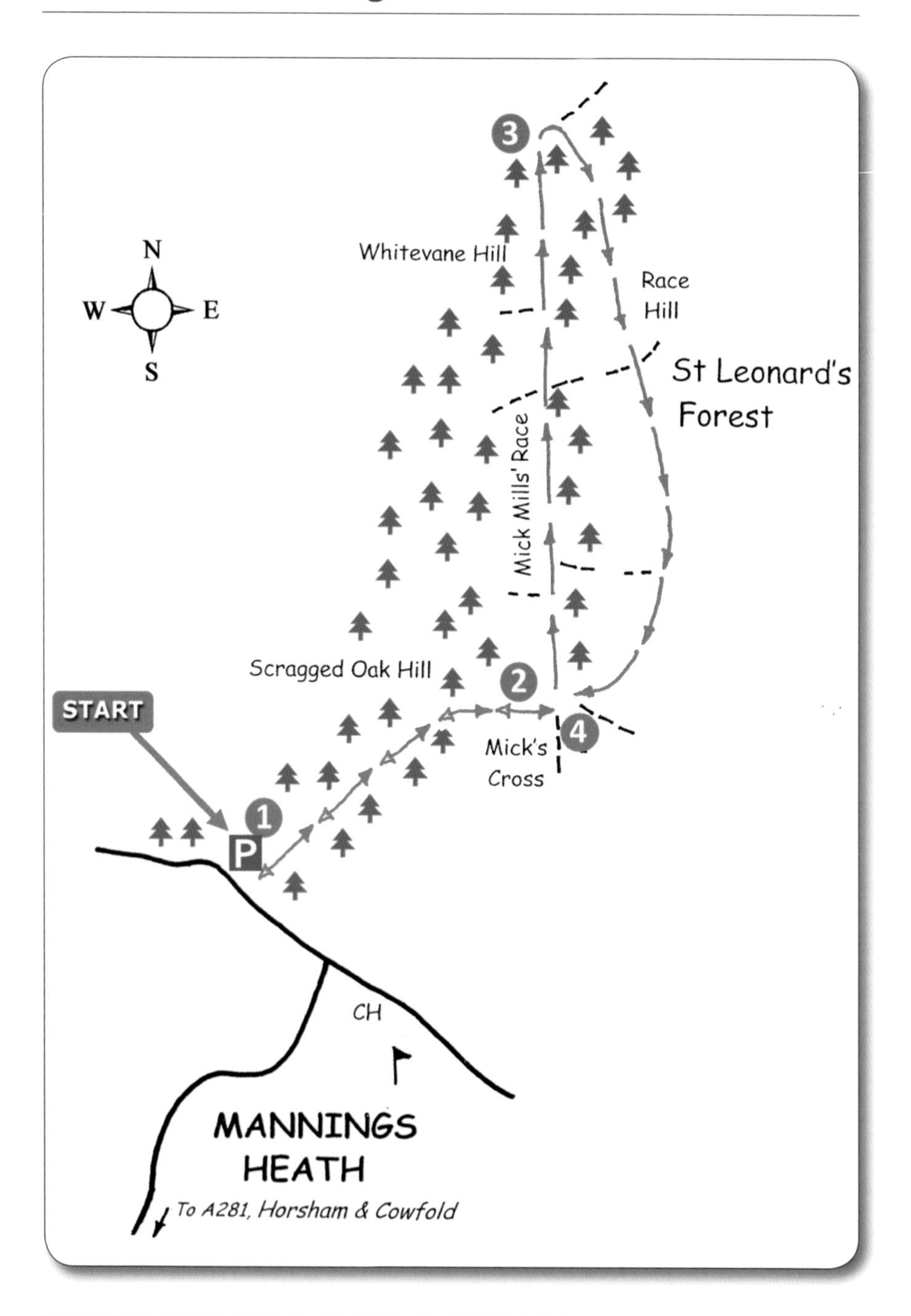
N
W
E
S
Whitevane Hill
Race
Hill
St Leonard's
Forest
Mick Mills' Race
Scragged Oak Hill
START
1
2
3
4
P
Mick's
Cross
CH
MANNINGS
HEATH
To A281, Horsham & Cowfold

2 This area is known as **Mick's Cross**. The way turns left here and you should follow the 1-mile-long broad track known as **Mick Mills' Race** through the forest ignoring all side paths and tracks. Finally, the track bends rightwards and meets a large spreading oak tree and a wonderfully carved seat depicting a dragon. There is a legend that the last dragon in England was slain here by St Leonard – another tall story!

3 Turn right here on another broad track on a downhill slope and again ignore all side paths. After heavy or prolonged rain this track can become a little muddy in places. Keep ahead when the track is joined by another from the left. The track eventually begins to rise and bend rightwards before ending at a T-junction by **Mick's Cross**.

4 Turn left here for 20 yards before turning right along the hard-surfaced track you walked earlier to reach the car park and the end of this lovely circuit.

Walking along Mick Mills' Race.

Clayton windmills and the South Downs Way

Ten-months-old Kit on a downland path.

This scenic circuit begins beside Jack and Jill, two old windmills that have been a landmark on this part of the South Downs above Brighton for many a year. The views from the entire route over the rolling downs are far-reaching and quite spectacular. The South Downs are popular with walkers, mountain bike riders and dog walkers, so your hound will have many chances of meeting and greeting other dogs and, more importantly, virtually the whole of the triangular route allows dogs to be off the lead. The way begins by heading south along downland paths through Rag Bottom where it meets the Sussex Border Path above Lower Standean. From here the route turns and heads off alongside open arable fields where it begins to climb slowly and easily back to the top of the downs and the South Downs Way for the last leg of this easy-to-follow route.

Terrain

Undulating.

Where to park

The free car park beside the Jack and Jill windmills. **OS map:** Explorer 122 Brighton and Hove (GR: TQ 303 134)

How to get there

The windmills are signed off the A273, just ½ mile south of the hamlet of Clayton. Follow a single track road to reach the car park beside the windmills. Clayton itself is 1 mile south of Hassocks.

Nearest refreshments

The **Jack and Jill Inn** in Clayton has a large, dog-friendly garden (dogs on leads) with lovely views towards the South Downs. There are some nice simple lunches available. ☎ 01273 843595

The Walk

1 From the car park entrance, go left on a stony track and pass the **Jack and Jill windmills**. Bear right at a fork and soon pass between paddocks and the buildings of **New Barn Farm**. Go ahead over a crossing track where, from

Dog factors

Distance: 3 miles.
Road walking: None.
Livestock: A small section of the route (see point 1) passes paddocks and an equestrian centre on a fenced path.
Stiles: None.
Nearest vets: Ark Veterinary Clinic, 44 Keymer Road, Hassocks BN6 8AR ☎ 01273 844399

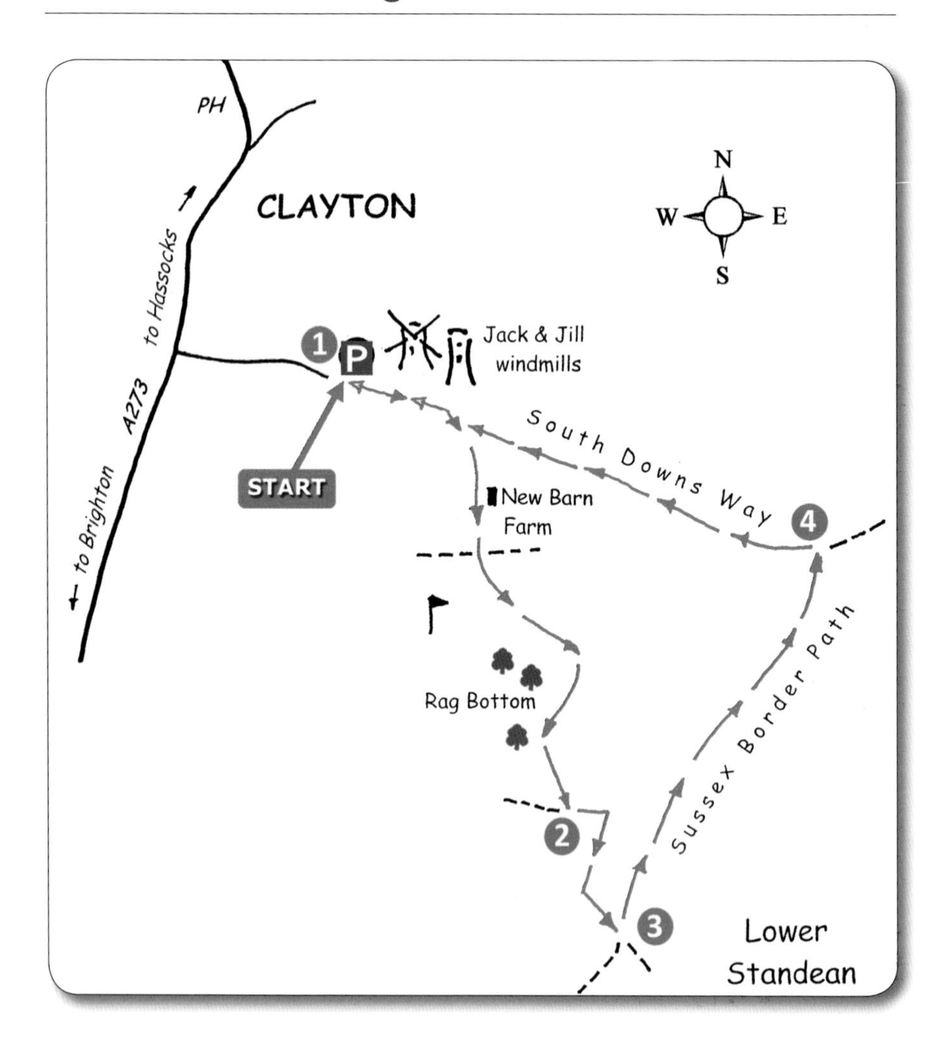

now on, dogs will have the freedom to roam. Follow this downland path as it continues alongside the manicured grounds of **Pyecombe Golf Club** and passes through **Rag Bottom**. After climbing a rise the path ends at a T-junction with a bridleway.

2 Turn left here along the bridleway to meet a tree line and a gate on your right. Pass through the gate and continue ahead to meet a second gate on your left. Go through this and continue along the right-hand side of a field to reach a third gate and a crossing path on the crest of the hill above **Lower Standean**.

3. This crossing path forms a part of the **Sussex Border Path** and you should now turn left along it. Continue up the well-trodden path, pass through a gate and press on up the downs until the path finally ends at the **South Downs Way**.

4. Now turn left along this well-trodden track, which offers more fantastic views, until the car park and the end of this easy-to-follow route is met.

A stunning view westward from the route over Pyecombe village that nestles in a fold of the South Downs.

Crawley Down and the Worth Way

The homeward path through arable fields.

This superb dog walk is surprisingly rural considering it begins in the sprawling village of Crawley Down and the longer version enters the suburbs of East Grinstead. After leaving Crawley Down via residential roads, the circuit soon plunges into the peaceful rural landscape as it follows the Worth Way path for one mile, where the option of the longer route begins. While the shorter route returns along the Sussex Border Path, the longer route swings north around Gullege, a centuries-old house and later, after passing the buildings of Imberhorne Farm, enters the outskirts of East Grinstead where it rejoins the Worth Way. Turning back, the path soon meets with the shorter version and now both routes follow the Sussex Border Path through scenic arable fields to return to Crawley Down.

Terrain

Fairly level.

Where to park

The small car park in Burleigh Way by the Royal Oak pub south of the village green or considerately at the roadside around the village. **OS map:** Explorer 135 Ashdown Forest (GR: TQ 346 374).

How to get there

Turn off the B2028 to reach Crawley Down, 1½ miles south of the A264 at Copthorne and 1½ miles north of Turners Hill. The car park is easiest found by following Grange Road to its end where Burleigh Way and the parking area will be visible on the right.

Nearest refreshments

The **Red Lion** pub tucked away in Lion Lane, Turners Hill is dog-friendly, offers a good selection of food and has a nice garden. ☎ 01342 715416

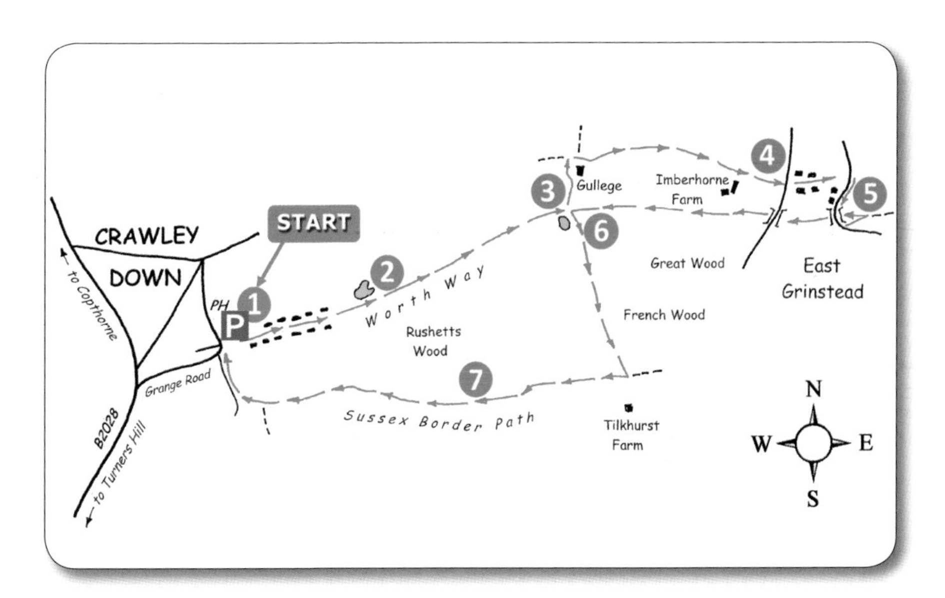

The Walk

1. With your back to the car park, turn left along **Burleigh Way** and soon turn right into **Copse Close**, at the end of which go ahead on a footpath. At the path end, go ahead along **Hazel Way** and at a left bend, go right into **Cob Close** to reach the **Worth Way** beside a scenic lake.

   The Worth Way follows the course of a dismantled railway – the Three Bridges to Tunbridge Wells Central Line. The line opened in 1855 and closed in 1967 as a result of the 'Beeching cuts'.

2. Continue ahead along the wide track, which offers easy walking for 1 mile and look out for a crossing path with a woodland pool on your right.

3. *For the shorter route, turn right here on the* ***Sussex Border Path*** *and follow the instructions from* ***point 6***. The longer route goes left on a well-trodden path that skirts an old house named **Gullege**.

   Gullege is a Tudor timber-framed house that was re-fronted in 1609 in the Jacobean style. The three chimneys date from Tudor times and it is believed the house was originally much larger.

   At a T-junction with a bridleway, turn right and pass the rear of the house. Press on along a wide concrete track, which offers fine views over the fields to the **North Downs** in the distance. Keep to this track and later pass the buildings of **Imberhorne Farm** before reaching **Imberhorne Lane**.

Dog factors

Distance: 3¼ or 5½ miles.
Road walking: ¼ mile of residential roads with pavements (½ mile for the longer route) and ½ mile private drive without pavement; 1 easy road crossing (3 on the longer route).
Livestock: None but maybe the occasional horse rider on the Worth Way.
Stiles: 5, all easy for large dogs.
Nearest vets: Copthorne Veterinary Clinic, Church Road, Copthorne, Crawley RH10 3RA ☎ 01342 713957

The Jacobean frontage of Gullege.

4 Cross the road and continue ahead on a bridleway between gardens to reach **Garden Wood Road**. Turn right alongside the road and, soon after passing a small green, the parapet of a bridge is reached. Here turn left on the path signed to the **Worth Way**.

5 There are steep steps on your immediate left that descend to the **Worth Way** but it is safer to continue along the rear of housing a little further before rejoining it. Turn left along the wide path and pass under **Garden Wood Road** and later under **Imberhorne Lane**. Now press on until the crossing path you met earlier is reached where you should now turn left.

6. Follow the signed **Sussex Border Path** through three arable fields. At the end of the third field, pass through the tree line and turn immediately right on the signed **Sussex Border Path**. Keep to the signed path and at a corner of the second field look out for the path as it goes right through a small wooded dell before entering the next field.

7. Maintain the general direction on the signed **Sussex Border Path** through fields to finally reach a tarmac drive beside the gates of **Burleigh House Farm**. Go right along the drive and at a small road junction turn right to soon rejoin the southern end of **Crawley Down**, the car park and the end of this good circuit.

The Worth Way offers easy walking.

By the waters of Ardingly Reservoir

Boats on Ardingly Reservoir.

This good short walk is ideal for young and old alike, whether they are our canine friends or we humans. Not only is the route picturesque but it is centred on a good picnic spot, which makes it ideal for an extended stay in this lovely place. Generally, during summer weekends there is plenty of activity taking place on the water to grab your attention or maybe you would prefer to take life easy and picnic awhile. The route begins at the large picnic area beside the scenic reservoir before following the water's edge to meet its turning point at a small lane. Soon the way heads into woodland and crosses a brook before climbing quite sharply to reach a quiet private drive, from the end of which it is just a short downhill stroll across a field to rejoin the water and the picnic spot.

Terrain

There is one short, sharp hill that will not trouble a person (or dog) of average fitness.

Where to park

The coin-operated on entry car park at Ardingly Reservoir. **OS map:** Explorer 135 Ashdown Forest (GR: TQ 335 286).

How to get there

Ardingly is on the B2028, south of Turners Hill and 5 miles north of Haywards Heath. From Ardingly, follow College Road south-west for 1 mile before turning along the signed drive to the reservoir.

Nearest refreshments

The large grassy area beside the dam of Ardingly Reservoir is a super picnic site. Alternatively, call in at the **Gardeners Arms** opposite the Ardingly Showground on the B2028, although it can get very busy if a show is on. Dogs are welcome inside and out. ☎ 01444 892328

The Walk

1. From the car park, make your way diagonally rightwards across the picnic site and up the bank of the dam to reach a well-trodden track at the water's edge.

Dog factors

Distance: 2 miles.
Road walking: 200 yards with limited verge (see point 2) plus ¼ mile of quiet private drive.
Livestock: None.
Stiles: 1, but with an opening gate beside it.
Nearest vets: Oathall Veterinary Group, 30 Oathall Road, Haywards Heath RH16 3EQ ☎ 01444 440224

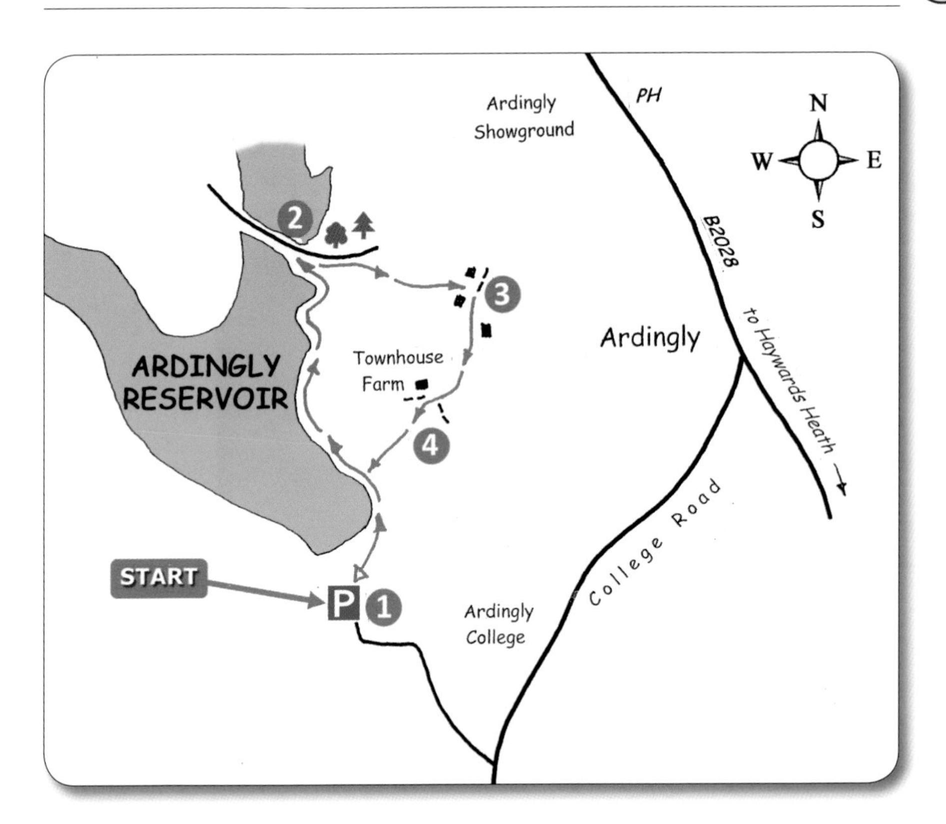

Now follow this track left alongside the water and remain on it until it ends at a small lane.

South East Water's Ardingly Reservoir, one of two it owns – the other is Arlington in East Sussex – combine to supply clean water to over two million homes. Ardingly Reservoir covers an area of 198 acres and was created in 1978, by damming a small tributary of the Ouse. It has a popular Activity Centre where you can enjoy sailing, windsurfing and canoeing. The Local Nature Reserve is home to a large number of bird species, including great crested grebe and kingfishers.

2 Turn right on the rising lane and in 200 yards, when opposite a small parking area on your left, fork right on a signed footpath and enter woodland. Soon cross a small footbridge over a woodland brook and ignore an indistinct path forking right. Our path goes straight uphill between pine trees for a short distance. At the top, the path becomes enclosed by fences and continues between houses to reach a private drive.

3. Turn right along this quiet drive and when the lane forks by **Old Knowles Cottage**, follow the right fork to reach the yard of **Townhouse Farm**. Ignore signed footpaths to left and right and go ahead towards **Ardingly Reservoir** visible in the distance.

4. Follow a well-trodden path across an arable field and at its end press on ahead to meet a stile and gate at a T-junction with the path walked earlier. Turn left now to soon rejoin the picnic area and the end of this delightful short walk.

Crossing a field on the return route with Ardingly Reservoir in the valley below.